S0-CCG-991

PersonalPatterns
by *Jinni*

FITTING PROBLEMS

And Their Corrections

Written and Illustrated by
Virginia (Jinni) Nastiuk

Also by Virginia Nastiuk

PERSONAL PATTERN DEVELOPMENT
Book I, Introduction to PatternMaking
and Design (Printed 1975 and 1976)
Book II, Introduction to Basic Design
(Printed 1975 and 1976)
Book III, A Collection of Favorite Designs
(Printed 1976)
(The above books are out of print)

PERSONAL PATTERNS By Jinni
A Manual for Perfect Patternmaking
(Printed 1986)

CHOOSING A PATTERN (Printed 1987)

● FITTING PROBLEMS And Their Corrections
(Printed 1987)

INTRODUCTION TO DESIGN (Printed 1987)

PANTS - Fit And Design (Printed 1987)

SKIRT - Fit And Design (Printed 1987)

First Printing 1987

ISBN# 0-942003-15-2

Copyright © 1987 by Virginia M. Nastiuk

All rights reserved. It is requested that no part of this book be
reproduced in any form without written permission from the author
except by a reviewer who may quote brief passages in a review.

Printed in the United States
Newman, Burrows Inc., Seattle, WA

Each "special subjects" book (ancillary) covers specific subject matter selected from PERSONAL PATTERNS By Jinni - A Manual for Perfect Patternmaking. And each subject has been expanded upon to contain additional informations that feature designing techniques.

The purpose of presenting this information in individual editions is for the convenience of the reader (whether teacher, dressmaker, student, professional or home sewer) to select the subject(s) of greatest interest and immediate importance--adding to the collection as the need arises.

CHOOSING A PATTERN

FITTING PROBLEMS AND THEIR CORRECTIONS

INTRODUCTION TO DESIGN

PANTS - FIT AND DESIGN

SKIRT - FIT AND DESIGN

and coming soon - - - -

BASIC DESIGN

ADVANCED DESIGN

KNITTING TO YOUR PERSONAL PATTERN

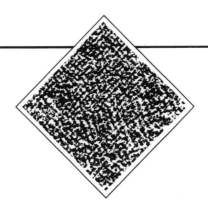

All About Jinni

Her grandfather was a tailor, European born and schooled in the fine art of clothing design, construction and fit. He passed his heritage on to his granddaughter Jinni, whose first simple stitches eventually grew into her own clothing design and manufacturing company. She is a Master Designer.

Jinni was especially interested in the fitting problems of those who sew and knit, whether for themselves and their families or for discerning clients. So she perfected her pattern developing skills and began the program of her dreams, "Personal Pattern Development" -- teaching tricks of the trade to women who want to achieve excellence in fit and to successfully design beautiful clothes. Today, Jinni continues to teach Master Design Courses, Design Classes, consult, and serve as Pattern Technical Director and Contributing Writer for "Sew It Seams" magazine.

Jinni wrote PERSONAL PATTERNS with one goal in mind, to pass her knowledge and expertise on to others, like you. From family sewing, dressmaking and designing, to manufacturing, consulting and teaching, Jinni's done it all. And now she shares it all by giving you her exclusive system for establishing perfect fit and developing PERSONAL PATTERNS.

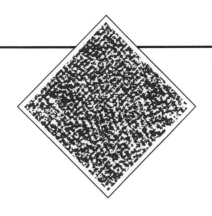

TABLE OF CONTENTS
FITTING PROBLEMS AND THEIR CORRECTIONS

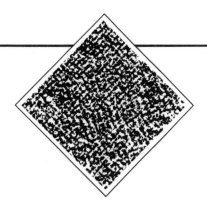

PREFACE

We are a wonderful and unique blending of cultures, traditions, and ethnic origins. We are all different from each other--the colors and textures of our hair and skin, our height, weight, and body proportions. Some of our differences affect the way our garments fit:

- Shoulder slope and pitch
- Armhole depth and width
- Leg and arm lengths and circumferences
- Muscle and flesh distribution
- Torso length and mass
- Bosom size
- Hip configuration--straight or A-line
- Waist configuration--thick or thin

Ready-to-Wear (RTW) manufacturers have always recognized that men come in a wide variety of sizes, shapes, and proportions. Witness that men's shirts are produced in numerous combinations of neck and sleeve measurements and their pants in numerous waist and inseam combinations. Women's clothing, however, comes in relatively few choices of sizes--small, medium, large, regular, queen size--with few if any variations available as to neck/sleeve or waist/hip/inseam combinations. Consequently, women must constantly search for a manufacturer whose proportions fit her body *and* her taste. This usually ends up in a compromise and ultimately a waste of precious time and scarce money. Some RTW manufacturers are beginning to address the phenomenon with their jeans that come in "26" sizes and brassieres that conform to shape, not just size.

However, whereas a man's physical structure enables RTW manufacturers to provide reasonably good fit by varying these combinations, the woman's body is much more complex and difficult to generalize. In addition, women's styles have been much more volatile and, consequently, it has been too expensive for the RTW industry to provide an adequate variety of size combinations.

For the average woman, the alternative is to sew her own clothes. Although this does provide more control over fit, style, etc., even here she receives inadequate data and little or no help addressing fitting problems. As a result, true fit has been possible only through custom-made clothing. Additionally, although it is not specifically stated anywhere, each pattern company develops patterns for a specific body type. This becomes obvious when one compares the finished garments of say Vogue, Burda, and McCall's (see CHOOSING A PATTERN for a detailed analysis of the differences between the pattern companies). Adding to the confusion are the multitude of "sure-fire," "quick-and-easy," "no-measure" methods that simply do not work--their authors being too inexperienced to deliver what they promise.

The Lucille Rivers system, for example, advocates taking only one measurement: the armhole size. A pattern is selected and through a series of fittings, altered to fit the wearer. I cannot help believing that this concept is one of the most ill conceived, misleading, inadequate schemes I have ever seen. And, yes, there are others!

Is it possible that the "magic," "easy," "instant," "no measuring," systems have contributed to the decline in home sewing; a lack of business for the young (uneducated and inexperienced) dressmakers; and the overall failure of the fabric business? Promoters are usually people who develop a theory but lack practical experience and expertise. They don't last very long in this business; but, however entertaining (or charming) their demeanor, they leave chaos and turmoil in their wake! Time is too short--Life is too precious to let promoters with gimmicky theories rob us of it.

Traditionally, bust, waist, hip, and back neck-to-waist length measurements have been used to establish a woman's pattern size--with differences in proportioning being addressed through Misses, Women's, Juniors, Miss Petite, and Half-Size figure types. However, critical areas such as shoulder slope and pitch, armhole depth and width, and distance between bust points, among others, have had to be generalized. Consequently, a majority of the women who sew have been sadly disappointed in the results of their efforts. Also, clear, simple instructions on how to handle these fitting problems are virtually non-existent. The issue is either avoided entirely by focusing on sewing techniques or it is made so rigid with rules and restrictions, that the home sewer becomes even more frustrated.

This book (and others in this series) fill that gap. By carefully following the steps outlined in this book, any sewer can develop a blueprint of any body for which he/she is sewing. This system enables a person to accurately define his or her body and to adjust for any irregularities, from the very common higher waistline to rounded backs, shortened arms or legs, etc.

There is nothing magical about this system. It takes a little time, a little patience, but the results are worth it. Remember, your goal is to have a garment that fits YOU, or whomever you are sewing for, not duplicate some ideal set of measurements, whether self-imposed or otherwise.

Unfortunately, until my system was developed, many of the fitting adjustments required to accommodate these idiosyncracies were largely unknown--certainly not available in print. In this book, each fitting problem is addressed individually so that you will gain greater understanding of the basic functions of apparel construction.

The key to successful dressmaking is the ability to identify and reconcile the differences between the shape of the pattern and the shape of the body for which it is intended. If we tilt a little here and there it is now possible to adjust the pattern to accommodate these variables and still develop a reliable basic pattern. The methods used for accomplishing this is also covered in this book.

Designing

Success is attainable not only to those who need help with fitting but to those who desire to express their own personalities and creativity.

You can create the garment you envisage--once fit has been attained, designing is a matter of practice and interest. When you combine perfect fit with your most flattering colors and styles in a garment of your choosing, you have found the answer to your clothing problems. You make an impressive statement about yourself before you utter a word: --that you know and like yourself--that you care about how you look--that you are in control.

I can't help wondering sometimes if we would not have been better off without the so-called conveniences of mass-produced patterns. In the past, patterns were made by a "Modiste" to fit each person as an individual; it was a way of life. Are we now just a moveable clothes rack? An easel for an artist's painting? Being manipulated into wearing fashions to extoll a designer's ego? If so, let us be the artist, the designer; when they fit perfectly, designing your own clothes can be tremendously rewarding.

The home sewer with an accurate personal pattern soon begins to look at clothes more objectively. She becomes more curious about how a garment is constructed so she can duplicate it at home. She attends sewing classes where she can place more emphasis on fine finishing details and tailoring classes to learn construction techniques.

There is an endless variety of fabrics and trims--or for that matter, even yarns for knitting. And if you want to make your own fur coat, hides and skins are available in nearly as many varieties. The tool that guarantees perfect fit for every endeavor is a personal pattern.

Who Will Benefit?

A great number of people wish it were possible to get a better fit--to just sit down and sew up something without the tedious ripping and refitting. This book is dedicated to those people. Whatever your interest in clothing construction--teacher, knitter, home sewer, professional--the personal pattern makes life easier. Once fit is established, you can devote your valuable time to methods of handling fabrics, application of finishing techniques, etc. If you are a sewing teacher, you will appreciate the accuracy attainable with this system.

If you are a student or a person with an inquiring mind and the engineering (technology) in the garment industry intrigues you, you will become more aware of drag and stress lines and begin to think in terms of attaining fit. **EVERY PERSON** is a subject for fit evaluation--what adjustments are necessary and what options are open to achieve a more pleasing appearance.

If you are a **professional dressmaker**, the accuracy of the personal pattern will excite you too. Not only does it make available to you the wider variety of fitting solutions, but the pattern itself will enable you to plan, design, and accurately make complete wardrobes through the simple, but vital application of Fit Coordination. It will help you to be more efficient because it greatly diminishes the need for multiple fittings; even the commercial patterns can be skillfully altered to fit your clients proportions and shape.

If you are a **home knitter** or a person who does charting for knitters, you will appreciate the personal pattern more with each design. The control for perfect fit of any garment is there and your valuable expertise can be used in duplicating all styles exactly. Owners of knitting machines with tracing aids have a distinct advantage over those who do charting because they can create lovely garments with the same precision as the home sewer.

Knitting machines hold such wonderful potential. Their technological development gives us the opportunity to knit in a day what in the past it has taken us weeks (even months) to do by hand. What an exciting new adventure!

Distance is no longer a problem for the **mother who sews and knits** from a personal pattern while her daughter is away at school or traveling. And then there is Aunt Bess in Faraway City who wants to make something nice. This time it will fit if you send her a copy of your pattern. Or how about that Hong Kong tailor you met on your last trip? He can do an even better job for you if he has a copy of your pattern from which to work. And you might take a copy along on your next trip so you can bring home enough yardage this time.

I am reminded of patterns I made for two women whose husbands were engineers. The men were fascinated with the concept of designing clothes and realized they needed a basic from which to accomplish this; but they did not know how to go about drafting a basic. The last I heard, these men were successfully styling their wives' clothing, and sewing them too! They called me a **"body engineer"** and the title has stuck. (Perhaps my engineering experience, limited as it was, has proven instrumental in developing this system.)

Special Women!

Several years ago, I was giving a seminar in Portland, Oregon. When it was over, a beautiful woman (who was seated at the time) began questioning me. After I assured her that this system would work for **any** body shape, she asked me to make a pattern for her so that she could make her own clothing. She told me of the many dressmakers who had failed to correct her fitting problems. She knew how to sew and reasoned that, if she could get "even one pattern" that fit well, changing colors and fabrics would give her enough variety in her wardrobe to satisfy her needs. She wanted something she could do for herself **immediately**.

And then she stood up (well, partially stood up). A crippling disease had so distorted her body that she could not stand straight or walk without a cane. Suddenly my mind was hit with the echoes of the reassuring statements my mouth had made only moments before: **"Regardless of shape--a pattern can be made that will fill any sewer's needs and desires and, yes, it will fit."**

How much time did it take? A long time. I remember that night very well. It took 3-1/2 hours, until about 2 a.m. Exhausted but exhilarated, I walked across the street to Patti Palmers apartment where I was staying with her and Susan Pletsch. It was a beautiful warm night in August and the moon was out.

A few months later, I was at the Double Tree Inn in the Southcenter area of Seattle. While walking through the lobby I heard a voice call out "Jinni? Virginia Nastiuk?" When I turned around I saw a very beautiful woman with a cane making her way toward me. It was good to see her and to hear about the exciting sewing projects she was doing. She had **designed and made** the chic garment she was wearing. It was truly perfect and a work of art! I was so very proud of her!

Reflecting back to this experience, I feel grateful now for these challenges--grateful for my exploring attitude that wouldn't let me rest until its search for answers to **Perfect Fit for Every Body** was satisfied.

I met Helen over the telephone when she called to ask questions about fitting. The next week she called again and asked me to come to her home in Fairmont, West Virginia to help her. The only time open was Thanksgiving week.

The airlines were very busy but I was able to get reservations on short notice and made arrangements to spend one week.

Helen is a lovely, gracious person. We became close friends instantly. She loves to sew; she has to sew in order to have anything to wear. And, like most of us, she has a lot of fabric on hand because she would buy a few more pieces for each sewing class she attended.

The result of her patience and attention to detail is a beautiful sewing technique; but it was done on garments that were never finished because they didn't fit. There were 14 garments in all and another 10 test shells in her closet that were unfinished. The muslin test shells were intended for establishing a basic pattern. She bought muslin by the bolt. When I saw all the confusion, anxiety, and frustration that inexperienced teachers had caused in her life, I was appalled and went to my room to "rest" and to contemplate what I had just witnessed. She had tried every system any promoter brought to the East Coast. Because Helen was so desparate, she would attend classes as far as 100 miles away only to be terribly disappointed again. So much time was spent on pattern alterations and muslins that, by the end of the scheduled course, the test shell still didn't fit, and again she had "nothing to wear."

Let's not get the impression that Helen's body is wierd or misshapen; because it is not. She is an attractive, 6 foot blonde with slender hips, erect shoulders, small waist, moderately full bosom, and graceful long arms that befit her height. According to commercial patterns, she was a tall version of size 18 on upper torso and a tall version of size 14 on the lower. One of the systems, among many, that failed her was the Lucille Rivers system.

Helen represents hundreds upon hundreds of my favorite people. She, they, you are the reason for my desire to document and publish my system. I want to share with people who sincerely desire **perfection**. Helen now has clothes that fit; she can now spend as much time as she wants to on the beautiful finishing details she enjoys without becoming entangled in the trauma of ripping and fitting and never completing what she starts.

Another lovely woman for whom I made a pattern has no use whatsoever of her hands or arms. Now her daughter designs and cuts everything out for her while she does all the sewing herself--operating the sewing machine with her feet while sitting on the floor. Can promoters guarantee her the total satisfaction and flawless designing results from their gimmicky theories? Can you imagine spending many hopeful hours making a lovely garment only to give it away because it didn't fit?

And yet another dear woman was struck by polio at the age of 18 years. It left her body disfigured and with arms that dangle at her sides. To our eyes they are not worth much more than paper weights.

I met Doris at a lecture on one of my first trips to Alaska. I drafted a basic pattern for her, reflecting on the experience with the lady in Oregon as I worked. With each trip to

Sitka or Juneau, Doris is there taking more classes. She stands beside a low table and swings each arm to get her hands onto it. Then she pushes and slides the paper and her basic pattern around, designing blouses, jackets, coats, and anything else she wants. By holding a pencil between two of her twisted fingers on the right hand, she drags the arm along to make faint and sometimes squiggly lines.

Doris designs and sews *ALL* of her clothing! She is always smiling and a joy to be with. What a wonderful person!

Being able to help these beautiful people has been a tremendous experience. They are an inspiration to me and have made me grateful for having a talent that I can share. I enjoy the challenge, but most of all I seem to come alive through such very SPECIAL people.

There are more Doris's and Helen's and beautiful women on canes who must be told that there is Hope and Honest Help out of their dilemmas.

There really is an answer!
We can prove it!
We do it every day!

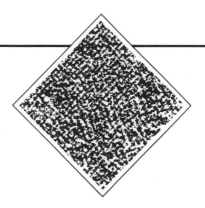

INTRODUCTION

A pattern is a guide, a means used to make a specific style of garment. The commercial pattern companies grade each style into many sizes; unfortunately, however, their patterns still do not fit us all. And, of course, they cannot possibly produce patterns for all the combinations of sizes that we come in. We are made of flesh and bone, varying in size depending upon our eating habits, vocational and recreational activities, and racial origins. Our faces do not look alike; how can we expect our bodies to fit into "look-alike" patterns?

Historically, commercial patterns were intended to expedite the home sewers task by providing a guide. However, over time people lost sight of this function and mistakenly began to believe that the patterns themselves were intended to fit--if they could only find the right one. Eventually the tail was wagging the dog; the pattern became the master rather than the guide. If the pattern did not fit, it was the sewers fault. **Her body** was too something: Too short waisted, too long waisted, too hippy, too flat chested, too broad shouldered, too narrow, etc. The pattern was right and she was misshapen or in some way inadequate.

Over and over again, I hear, "I have such terrible sewing problems." But, when we discuss these sewing problems, invariably we find that our sewer really does not have problems with sewing--she has problems with fitting. She really loves to sew if sewing were all she had to do. And so it is actually the ripping and fitting that is discouraging. Ripping and fitting costs us precious time which could be spent on more pleasant pursuits.

I have yet to measure a body that will fit a specific commercial size perfectly. If yours does, you are very rare. Rare? Yes, because the pattern companies are not standardized within their sizes and are even inconsistent with fit within their own brands. For instance, I have tested different pattern numbers (same brand, same size) that looked exactly alike on the outside of the envelopes only to discover that the size and proportion of the patterns did not conform.

No wonder the home sewer has so much difficulty deciding on which brand and which size to buy.

This writing is not intended to discredit the pattern industry, nor is it meant to criticize you because you do not fit garments made from their patterns. The pattern companies do an outstanding job of bringing us the latest in fashion, and the accompanying instruction sheets are useful. I recommend using their services whenever we can. But, in order to do this successfully, most of us need to understand more about pattern sizes and how they differ from our requirements. (See Chapter I, "Inter-Brand Comparisons," CHOOSING A PATTERN.)

Fabric is a variable and a factor on how your garment will fit. A corduroy dress will not fit the same as a jersey dress even though they are cut from the same pattern. Your choice of style for a particular fabric makes a difference.

One example of style/fabric incompatibility would be combining chiffon or a very stretchy knit with Princess styling. The weight of the fabric will always pull along the seam lines, creating unsightly drag lines. So why fight it, simply do not combine them--use woven fabric for the princess styling.

The characteristics of knits are compatible with the raglan style--the stretchiness allows the fabric to mold over the round of the shoulder. In addition, in the raglan style, it is not necessary to stabilize the shoulder seam, as may be necessary if a set-in sleeve pattern were used. Often, in fact, the stabilizing may hold the seam from stretching out but the surrounding areas may still stretch and be the cause of undesirable puckers and drag lines.

People who knit, either by hand or with knitting machines, benefit greatly from choosing a compatible yarn and pattern. They are creating a fabric--shaping each piece of the garment exactly to size and assembling it without seam allowances. A lot of time and effort goes into making a garment in this manner-- what if it does not fit the body for which it was intended? The wary knitter will make a large test swatch in order to check the hand and gauge before embarking on such an ambitious project.

Stable knits, however, combine nicely with the princess styling or with the set-in sleeve. They are usually made of double knit construction--controlled stretch. I have (and possibly you have, too) sewn on knits that have no stretch at all. The fabric manufacturers have many ingenious methods of making cloth.

People who crochet are producing yet another type of fabric-- expending energy and using their precious time and talents on to create a useful garment. They have great expectations that their hand-crafted item will comfortably fit the body for which it was intended. They all have one thing in common--the expectation and the hope of fit.

People who do needle point will find their work very rewarding when made into an item they can wear. When these people are assured of good fit through simple basic knowledge of it, their creative minds produce endless variations of wearable art.

Is fit personal? Is there such a thing as perfect fit? Though fit means something different to everyone, if a garment is comfortable when worn for the use for which it was intended, it can be said to fit. Some of us like clothes that feel snug and others prefer them loose; to that extent, **fit is personal.** Of course, to be comfortable, it must have the correct proportioning for all of our body parts. With a basic pattern of our own body, a sort of blueprint like an architect uses, we would have the freedom to diversify the styles and snugness or looseness in complete confidence.

THE MISSING LINK

FIT is the missing link (the key) to successful and satisfying apparel construction regardless of a person's shape, size, or sex. Therefore an accurate blueprint of the body (which is what the personal pattern represents) provides these successful results. And until now, the sewer or craftsperson was at the mercy of the limited experience of those people who simply did not even consider fit, but merely design.

Is there truly a One-Size-Fits-All?, or a Magic Fit?, or a Fuss Free?, or a Quick and Easy?, or a Measure Free?, or an American Way pattern that is guaranteed to fit everyone?; even with the alteration techniques they offer? --Of course not!!--

The problem of fit has always existed. The approach to eliminating the problem has been changed, but it has not been the success story that we are led to believe. For a few of those who sew, there may be a specific size and brand that has fulfilled their apparel needs, but it is evident that problems still exist with the commercialized systems; otherwise, why are there thousands of closets and drawers with unfinished garments....??

When a pattern fits, when control and promise of a successful garment every time are a reality, more people sew, buy sewing machines and tracing aids for their knitting machines, buy fabric, and gain confidence because of the satisfying results.

Sizing Changes In Patterns

Did "Brand X" pattern fit before but not any more? This is quite possible. The pattern companies change their sizing and proportioning occasionally (Vogue did in 1976, McCall's did in 1980, and Burda did in 1982). But another factor should be noted here; expressed very well in a letter from a confused woman who has sewn for many years. She stated that she "always used a size 12 pattern and it still fits fine except in the **bust, waist, and hips,**" and she wanted to know what to do about it.

Because she wore a size 12 pattern for fifteen years, does not mean that she is the same proportions or shape today (even though she still weighs 123 pounds). Flesh and muscle shapes change to suit the needs of different physical activities. Operations such as mastectomies alter the muscle shapes that hole our bone structure in a particular posture. Illness can also have a crippling effect. However, aging is the most common factor:

Bosom is lower; Abdomen may be bloated and waistline higher; Back is more rounded and neck angles forward; Shoulders pitch forward; Buttocks are flatter.

The people who today experience the real pleasures from their sewing efforts are those who own a reliable basic pattern. For some it may be no more than one pattern from which they have made a successful garment and, through ingenuity and practice, developed a series of variations--color, texture, fabric. The result of their handiwork truly is "fuss-free," "measure-free," "quick and easy." To those who have not yet experienced this pleasure, it may seem like magic; but there is no magic to it--it's all so very simple!

FOR THE PROFESSIONAL

For the professional, whose time is valuable, there is no greater investment than the productive application of her expertise. When people are willing to pay for your work and advice, but the job takes longer than anticipated, you are faced with a choice: 1.) charge more at the risk of losing a customer, or 2.) absorb the cost, thereby being underpaid for your time and talents. Of course, when the error is of our own doing, we must absorb the cost. Many of us have spent many hours correcting problems without charge; and we have even reduced our price for the client who changed her mind or weight. However, when we spend hours fussing with an aspect of sewing over which we should have control, we cannot rightly bill our clients nor can we really afford to absorb the cost. And FIT is one area that, as a professional, we should have mastered.

There are areas over which we sometimes have not had the control we anticipated from a commercial pattern. Trying to fit after the cutting was done or leaving outlets (extra seam allowances), which requires that the pieces of a garment be pinned together on the client, are all too often futile. These systems must be recognized as counterproductive.

Dressmakers and designers who work with a client through the means of a Personal Pattern find they have the perfect tool that gives them better productivity and freedom. Freedom from confusion. Freedom from dogma. Freedom of choice. It gives them total control in every aspect of fit for a client: total control over the time element, which in turn controls the pricing structure and overhead operating expenses. Your time is valuable!

What establishes your credibility? Is it the easy, confident and reassuring manner you portray as you go about your work? Less time spent by the client in a fitting session is important and impressive to her and makes you worth more money. Does it make sense that truly busy and important people (who are usually the ones who can afford your talents) have the time to spend on multiple alteration fittings? Does it make sense that the really rich and famous might have a Personal Pattern (however it was contrived) hanging in a designers' workshop? Can you imagine Nancy Reagan, Jackie Onassis, or for that matter the Queen of England, being required to return to a salon for "16" fittings?

How long do you think such a salon would maintain its clientele or prestige? Regardless of the price of the fabric they put into a garment or fashion trend at the moment, isn't FIT the final test? Does the wearer make an impressive silent statement about herself/himself through her/his apparel? Being impeccable includes great fit and responsibility for the client's impression rests squarely upon the shoulders of the designer and staff.

If your livelihood is dependent upon continuing education, advanced knowledge and skill in your craft, the information in Chapter II of CHOOSING A PATTERN or in Appendix-C, PERSONAL PATTERNS By Jinni - A Manual For Perfect Patternmaking, is a valuable study of several commercially produced patterns. If you sew for your client by using this medium, you will see how it seriously (for good or for bad) influences the efforts you are presenting to your client; yes, it may even prove to be limiting.

Stretching your realm of knowledge leads to the exercise of creativity and on into the strength of confidence. A result that you will enjoy in yourself.

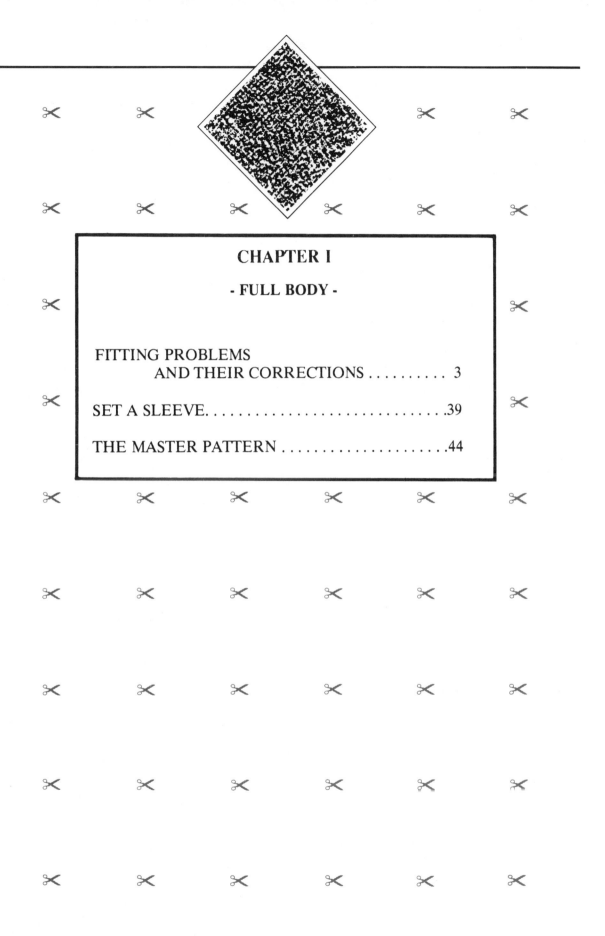

CHAPTER I

- FULL BODY -

CHAPTER I

--FULL BODY--

FITTING PROBLEMS AND THEIR CORRECTIONS

This chapter outlines common fitting problems and their corrections.

The first part, Balancing Act, identifies those areas of a drafted basic that might need fine tuning. The second part, fitting problems, etc., deals with problems that may arise if a commercial basic was used. It might be useful in identifying problems with fashion garments as well.

This is where all your drafting effort begins to pay off because your find tuning adjustments are much simpler and easier to identify and make than with a commercial pattern.

BALANCING ACT

If the need for a personal pattern exists at all, the "balancing act" is the exciting next step. It is vital that the muslin be sewn accurately in order to make accurate adjustments on the pattern. The life-long benefits of a Personal Pattern are so far-reaching that, when this final act is performed, the awareness that all potential problems have been addressed and need NEVER arise again leaves one with a good feeling of freedom and confidence. The exciting adventures into designing are endless because the way is made simple and easy.

These are important areas that directly influence future designing. Through this balancing act, you will establish:

1. The positioning of the **bust darts** as well as the balance between them.

2. The width of the **back bodice** balanced to the width of the front bodice--particularly the shoulder-tip to shoulder-tip.

3. Proper balance between bodice and sleeves in forward curve of **armhole**.

4. The proper balance between the front and back bodice at the **shoulder line**; eliminating a gapping neckline.

5. Proper balance between the shoulder seam and the shape of the **crown** on the sleeve.

6. An understanding in the application of **logic** in order to achieve perfect fit for anyone, regardless of shape, sex, age, or size.

1. **Bust Darts**. Bust darts are properly balanced when there are no drag or stress lines. Lines such as those shown in Fig. I,1a, often mean the dart under the bust is not wide enough. If you rip out the side seam, the amount of adjustment may be determined by pinning most or all of the excess fabric into the dart under the bust--some may need to be put into the dart at the side as well. However, the amount of fabric put into the dart under the bust will need to be replaced at the side seam.

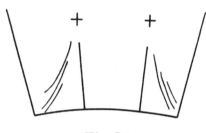

Fig. I,1a

On the other hand, if the drag lines point in the opposite direction and look like the illustration in Fig. I,1b, it means there is too much fabric in the dart. If you rip the side seam, the dart, and the front waistline, the stress is relieved and the dart can be narrowed. The excess fabric is pinned out at the side seam.

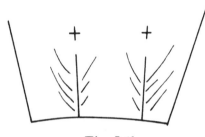

Fig. I,1b

2. **Back Bodice**. Proper balance is achieved when the amount of bustline ease is distributed almost evenly around the body. When the back appears loose, and the front appears tight, it means the side seam and armhole are positioned too far forward. (The proposed adjustment is more easily determined when the sleeve is removed.)

Two things may have combined to cause this:
- The back darts are too wide.
- The underarm measurement was too long. (This is the most likely cause.)

The broken line in Fig.I,2 indicates the correction. The excess fabric is removed from the back--extra fabric is added to the front.

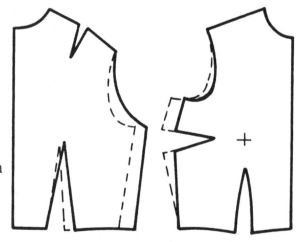

Fig. I,2

3. **Armhole**. Proper balance in the forward curves of the armhole is necessary to prevent stress and/or eliminate excess fabric across the chest; the latter would possibly create a cutting feeling in the armpit. Figure I,3 illustrates the adjustment for relieving stress. Without pulling at the fabric in any way, add extra fabric to the front armhole **OR**, if the problem is excess fabric, trim away excess fabric as shown by the broken line in Fig. I,4a.

Try to avoid "overfitting" and getting the muslin so snug that the ease amounts are eliminated. In viewing this area a small bubble effect should remain forward along the armhole, beginning about 1-1/2" to 2" *(3.7cm to 5cm)* below the shoulder point and extending into the underarm curve but not continuing through to the underarm seam.

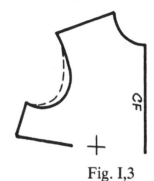

Fig. I,3

Fig. I,4a

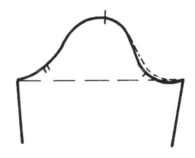

Fig. I,4b

After re-sewing the sleeve into the adjusted bodice curve lines, the cap may appear to be a bit snug across the crown. Figure I,4b shows the adjustment that may be advisable, remembering the necessary slight bubble effect.

4. **Shoulder Line**. Improper balance between the front and back bodice parts at the shoulder line is recognizable by stress and tightness across either the front shoulder-tip to shoulder-tip or the back shoulder-tip to shoulder-tip. The remedy is to add fabric to the appropriate piece.

More often the stress shows up across the front. Rip the shoulder seams, and, if necessary, trim the front neckline lower; also, partially remove the sleeve from the armhole through the crown area of the back side and through the front crown forward to include the notch near the armpit.

Fig. I,5

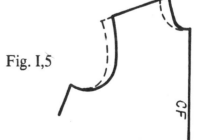

Hold (or tape) the back of garment to the body and lay the front smoothly against the body towards the shoulder line. Pin the shoulders together being careful not to create stress again nor to create a gapping neckline. Adjustment is shown in Fig. I,5 by the broken line.

5. Shoulder Seam. Proper balance for the shoulder seam is initially determined by the position of the reference dots placed on the body for accurate measuring. As stated earlier, the dot on the shoulder bone **MUST** be centered and not placed toward the back. There will be a time in your designing when manipulating the seam is desirable, as on a raglan jacket or coat; however, if the seam is not placed correctly initially, the raglan style cannot be satisfactorily developed from it. Adjust it by adding to the one part what is removed from the other as shown by the broken line in Fig. I,6.

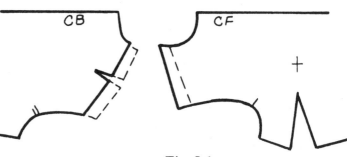

Fig. I,6

Look for balance on the cap of the sleeve too. Besides moving the dot forward on the crown, it may be necessary to remove some excess fabric from the back side (ease for comfort and movement is needed so allow some bubbling to remain). The front sides of the crown should have very little or no bubble at all (but show no signs of being too tight either).

The sleeve adjustment is illustrated by the broken line in Fig. I,7.

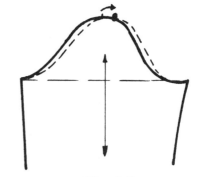

Fig. I,7

Although the following fitting problems and corrections can occur with any pattern, they are more likely to appear when the basic is developed from a commercial pattern. Therefore, the purpose for this section is to provide answers mainly for those of you who elected to use a commercial pattern rather than to draft your own.

As you read through and study the various problems, you may recognize alterations that you wondered about but were afraid to try. I hope you will indeed try the various techniques and experience the thrill of satisfaction in your successes.

Some theories propose that, if the bustline is a particular measurement, the back and even the arm measurement can be predicted. However, practical application shows that this is not true. On a woman's body particularly, the front proportions will vary considerably, not being related to the shape or measurement of any other part of the torso or limbs. There simply is no relationship between them. The fitter should address each area separately so that alterations are aimed at reducing the amount of excess fabric, or providing extra fabric, where necessary.

BUSTLINE WRINKLES

These wrinkles and the sagging fabric appearance occur when there is too much fabric across the front, from side to side and from shoulder to waist. This person probably wears a brassiere with a size A cup. (See illustration of problems in Fig. I,8a.)

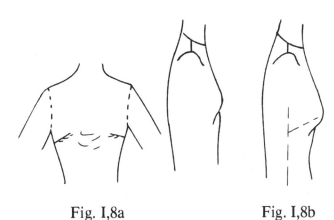

Fig. I,8a   Fig. I,8b

The profile of an average body is shown in Fig. I,8b. Commercial patterns are made to fit the size B brassiere cup size.

To correct the muslin:

1. Rip the stitching from waist to underarm, allowing the armhole to remain together.

2. Rip the stitching from the bust dart at the side seam and press out the creases of the stitching line. With the muslin hanging straight down from the bust, pin the side bust dart to the desired width. Cut the excess fabric from the lower edge of the bodice. (See Fig. I,8c.)

Fig. I,8c

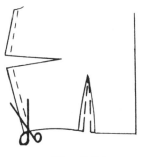

Fig. I,8d

3. The underbust darts may have to be made narrower and 1/2" *(1.2cm)* or more may have to be trimmed from the side of the front bodice. (See Fig. I,8d showing the broken line as the correction.)

BULBOUS BOSOM (DD, EE, GG)

Stress lines occur between the bust points
due to insufficient fabric. Also, drag lines
across the back are produced because of the
improper bust dart size. Solutions presented
here are unique for the particular "bulbous"
shape on this womans body. Figure I,9a
illustrates possible body shape.

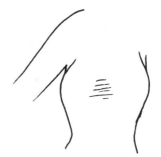

Fig. I,9a

Good fit for this person cannot be achieved with the customary straight stitching line on
the side bust dart; also, the point of the dart cannot be press-shaped into a curve suitable
for this bosom. (See Fig. I,9b for illustrations of three areas of fitting adjustments.)

1. "A" in Fig. I,9b shows **concave** shaping
(slight): to keep the fabric lying smoothly
against the small rib cage underarm.

2. "B" in Fig. I,9b shows **convex** shaping: to
fit around the fullness of the side bust
(preventing the gapping armhole that may
occur when sewing the conventional straight
dart).

3. "C" in Fig. I,9b shows a small **straight**
dart, usually rather slim if it is needed at all.
The length is adjusted appropriately.

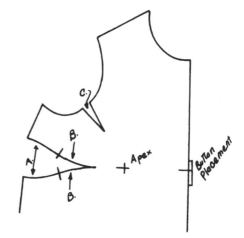

Fig. I,9b

Because a dart shaped like the above often
requires special handling and trimming when
used on bulkier fabrics, the option of a
seam has proved more successful. The end
result in coats or jackets particularly is that
shaping and adjustments may be made more
accurately, without fussing with the point of
a dart. The seam is opened and pressed over
a dressmakers ham. (See Fig. I,9c.)

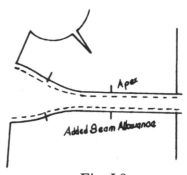

Fig. I,9c

ADJUSTING FOR THE GROWING BODY

Mothers who have invested the little time it takes to develop a pattern for their growing girls have found it to be well worth the effort. Garments can be completed confidently and without spending time in fittings except to decide the hem length. Copies of the patterns are helpful for aunts and grandmothers to have too. When they want to make gifts, there is always the reliable pattern to turn to.

Altering the pattern for a maturing girl is similar in principle to the bodice adjustments on the previous pages.

Generally, growth to the upperarm and back is minimal compared to that occurring in the front upper torso, i.e., the bosom. The girls personal pattern can easily be altered to reflect the body's growth.

The first indication of fitting problems will show up as folds at the armpit and a snugger-than-comfortable appearance across the bosom.

Initially, the pattern might resemble the outline shown in the solid line and labeled "A." The next change may resemble the broken line which is labeled "B." The final change may look like the dotted line "C."

"A" shows that a bust dart is not needed for this immature body. Also notice that the armscye has only a small amount of shaping.

"B" shows a high bust dart and apexes that relatively close together. Button placement is now important; one should be directly between the apex points. The overall length from shoulder to waistline increases and the armscye takes on more shape, i.e., the armscye point is raised an amount equal to half the bust dart width.

"C" shows how the final change may appear; longer from shoulder to waist, lower apex, wider dart, more width from side to side, and more shaping of the armscye.

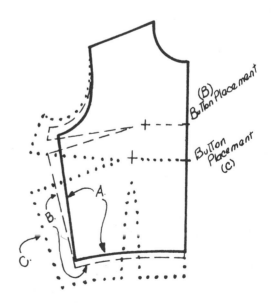

Fig. I,10

For further explanation of the purpose in shaping the armscye, see FOLDS AT THE FORWARD ARMPIT.

RESTRICTED REACH

When you reach forward, does your hemline come up or your blouse pull out from the waistband? When wearing a sweater or coat over a dress or blouse does the front bunch up across your chest? When you are driving, does the underarm of your dress or blouse seem tight so that your reach is restricted? These problems have one common cause: the armhole is cut too deep.

It is commonly, and wrongly, thought that if the reach is restricted, the armhole should be cut deeper; but the opposite (shortening the armhole depth) is the correct remedy. The commercial patterns are generally 1/2" to 3/4" *(1.2cm to 2cm)* too deep for most bodies (see Measurement Tables in CHOOSING A PATTERN). Stretch & Sew is one of the more extreme.

Notice in Fig. I,11a that the armhole depth of the pattern reflects the measurement of the body plus 5/8" *(1.6cm)* to allow for ease and room for the seam allowance to stand up.

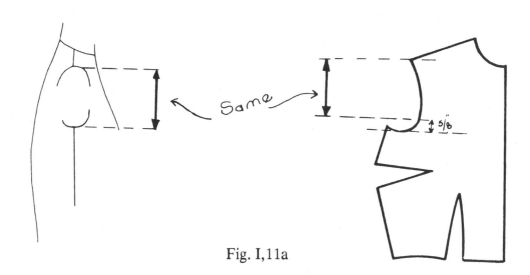

Fig. I,11a

To correct the muslin:

1. Rip the stitching at the underarm curve.

2. Baste a piece of fabric to both the bodice and the sleeve parts. When the underarm seam is correct, the cut edge of the seam will gently touch (but not cut into) the flesh of the armpit. The seam allowance around the armscye of the bodice and the cap of the sleeve should be only 3/8" *(1cm)* wide. (See "Set a Sleeve" and Fig. I,11b.)

The corrections may look about like this:

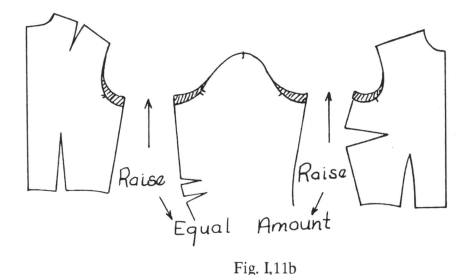

Fig. I,11b

There are other factors that contribute to sleeve fitting problems:

a. Repeated stitching causes the armhole to become smaller and may even produce puckering along the seam line.

b. Allowing the fabric to feed into the needle on its own can produce tight stitching and, in turn, cause puckering. The curves especially should be stretched moderately as they are sewn.

c. Loosely woven or stretchy knit fabrics seem to grow when cut into the shape of the armhole. Cutting the armhole smaller (as shown in Fig. I,11b) will prevent this problem. If the armhole is then too snug, it can easily be trimmed out to your comfort.

d. Seam allowances that are too wide tend to cause a distortion in the appearance along the lower curves of the armscye. A proper evaluation of the sleeve fit cannot be made while wide seam allowances remain. Trim before fitting. (See "Seam Allowance Analysis" and "Set a Sleeve".)

SLEEVE CAP WRINKLES

These wrinkles occur along the back cap of the sleeve. (See Fig. I,12a.) There may also be stress lines along the front cap extending down into the forward sleeve. Often there is stress across the upper back (neck and shoulders) accompanied by gapping at the front neckline.

Why is this problem more visible on some bodies than on others? Because the front part of the shoulder bone is pitched forward; probably caused by a rounded back. A pattern for this body must have more width across the upper back and less across the front. The sleeve cap needs more forward shaping in the crown in front of the shoulder dot and less to the back side of the crown.

Fig. I,12a

With the exception of Burda, the commercial pattern companies design for a body that looks like Fig. I,12b. This shows a straighter back and an arm that hangs very straight. Notice in Fig. I,12c that the sleeve is symmetric. Except for the notches to indicate joining to the bodice, it may be difficult to differentiate Front from Back. By comparing **Burda** to **Butterick,** it is plain to see Burda's proportioning is more suitable for the body structure appearing somewhere between the two extremes shown here.

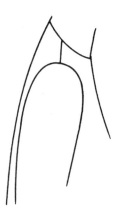

Fig. I,12b

To correct the muslin:

1. Rip the stitching along the sleeve cap down to the notches (front and back), allowing the armpit to remain stitched.

2. Rip the stitching along the shoulder seam.

3. With the muslin on, smooth the fabric across the chest. Pin and baste the shoulder seam to the desired fit, filling in at the side of the front neck as needed.

Fig. I,12c

4. Baste a strip of fabric along the bodice back armhole. Mark the desired armhole sewing line and trim the excess from the front armhole.

5. Pin the sleeve cap along the marked armhole line, taking a little of the excess bubble from the back side of the cap. Fill in the space above the sewing line forward of the shoulder dot.

NOTE: Care should be taken in reducing the bubble at the back of the cap; most people are inclined to fit the sleeve cap too smoothly. Some fullness is necessary for comfort and mobility.

The corrections to the pattern may look similar to those below:
(The shaded area and broken lines represent the corrections.)

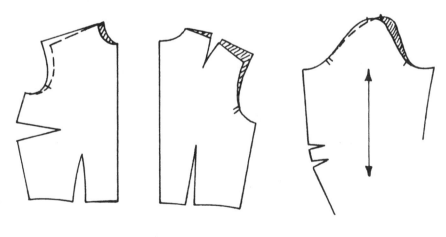

Fig. I,12d

FOLD AT FORWARD ARMPIT

A correctly designed garment should fit smoothly from the shoulder downward across the sides of bust to the waistline and not have a fold. There are exceptions in styling however, such as the Kimomo or Dolman, where a fold is unavoidable.

The fold in Fig. I,13a is seen on a garment that has no bust dart. However, it may also be seen if a.) the bust dart is not large enough and/or b.) the front armhole is cut too deep in relation to the back armhole depth.

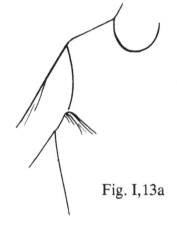

Fig. I,13a

If it seems that the bust dart is adequate, then try raising the front armscye point and armpit curve as shown in Fig. I,13b noting the broken line. Restitch the side seams beginning at the armpit--trim away the excess fabric at the side front of the bodice.

Fig. I,13b

To correct the muslin:

1. Rip the side seam from the armpit to the waistline.

2. Pin in the excess fabric to form a dart (or to enlarge the present one). Note that in most cases the width of the dart adjustment will be equal to the width of the fold and/or the amount of rise needed in the armpit.

3. Add a piece of fabric to fill in the armpit area and to reshape the curve as shown in Fig. I,13b.

NOTE: Puckers at the armpit can be caused by inexperience in setting sleeves, i.e., if the seams are too wide and the seam is sewn the wrong direction, then puckers are a predictable result!

ARMHOLE AND BACK WRINKLES

These wrinkles appear when the pattern does not duplicate the body shape; the bust dart is at fault, needing adjustment to accommodate the bosom. There is excessive fabric resulting in folds that begin at the Apex and extend into the back area, and, depending upon the size of the bosom, even extending across the entire back of the garment.

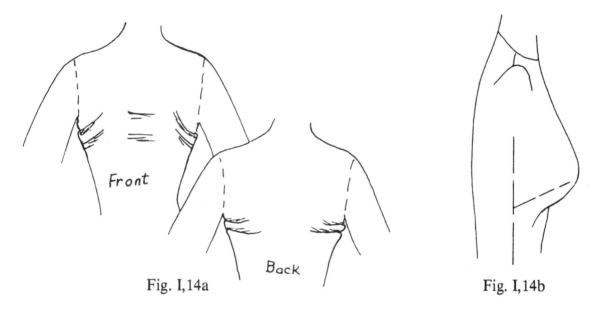

Fig. I,14a   Fig. I,14b

A profile of the body in Fig. I,14b illustrates how it may look with a size D cup on the brassiere.

To correct the muslin:

1. Rip the stitching from waist to armpit.

2. Rip the stitching across the front waistline. With the muslin hanging straight down from the Apex, pin the side bust dart to the desired effect. Pin a strip of fabric along the back bodice side seam and pin the front bodice onto it--adjusting upward or downward to establish desired armscye fit. Add a strip to the waistline of the front bodice and mark the corrected waist stitching line. (See Fig. I,14c for illustration of pattern changes.)

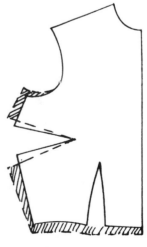

Fig. IV,14c

Burda Pattern Co. seems more successful in their approach to addressing correct fit for the body with the larger bosom than any of the other pattern companies. However, the changes **McCall's** made to their basic in 1980 appears to have at least reduced their previous bustline/armhole problem--perhaps giving total correction for many!

NOTE: Beside the above alteration, the underbust darts may need to be made wider or shorter and possibly moved outward to a position directly below the Apex. (See the broken line in Fig. I,14d.)

By now you may have realized that the corrections were done only to the front and nothing was done to the back.

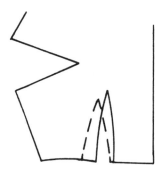

Fig. I,14d

BACK WRINKLES

This problem occurs on any body (male or female) that has a more rounded back. They may also have a flatter buttocks and their back waistline may dip lower while the front is higher.

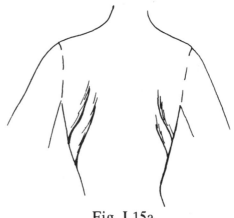

Fig. I,15a

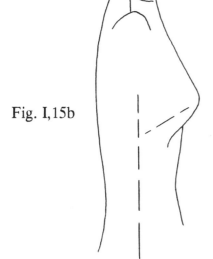

Fig. I,15b

A profile of the body that experiences back wrinkles is shown in Fig. I,15c. As you can see, the back is longer than the front; therefore extra length is needed on the pattern from the back of the neck to the waistline, less length in the front bodice. Because of this tilted waistline more length is needed on the front skirt from waist to hem and less length on the back skirt.

The profile of the average body may look like the one in Fig. I,15b. As you can see, there is quite a difference between these two bodies. The rounded-back illustration is drawn with more curve in order to emphasize the problem area.

Fig. I,15c

To correct the muslin:

1. Rip the stitching along the shoulder seam; but allow the shoulder tip to remain together.

2. Rip the stitching from the side seams beginning at the underarm, to the hem or waist; but allow the armhole to remain together.

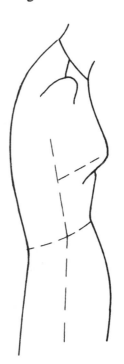

3. Drop the back down until the wrinkles disappear. Pin a strip of fabric along the front shoulder; making it wide enough to pin the back shoulder at the desired position.

4. Measure the space at the neck edge of the back bodice and correct the pattern accordingly as shown by the shaded area in Fig. I,15d.

5. Pin a strip of fabric along the front side seam. Smoothly lay the back muslin down the body half way between the side and the spine, pinning in the center back seam, beginning at about the shoulder blades and continuing down to the hem.

6. Pin the back side seams onto the strip. Mark the corrections onto the pattern. For the one-piece garment, the back will look about like the one in Fig. I,15d.

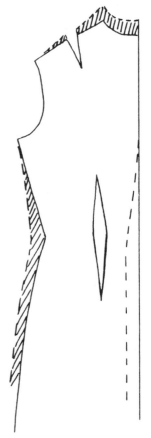

Fig. I,15d

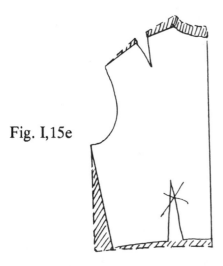

Fig. I,15e

Some changes may also be necessary at the front. Depending upon the extent of the back curvature, there may be too much fabric in the chest area between the shoulder line and bustline. Pin out the excess across the chest--or it may be sufficient to cut the neckline lower. (See Fig. I,15f.)

The correction of the two-piece (fitted) back will look about like that shown in Fig. I,15e. The dart at the waistline is omitted in order to de-emphasize the roundness of the back; gather the bodice onto the skirt for softer detailing.

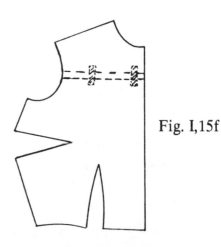

Fig. I,15f

NOTE: Failure to recognize the results of unsuitable patterns in this area leaves a lot of the sewing population frustrated. The need for the back shoulder and neckline alterations is clearly seen on the majority of people and nearly all elderly men and women--the hems of their coats or jackets are shorter in back and protrude. When we look at the sides, the garment side seams hang (swing) toward the back and the front hemline dips longer.

Sewers are not the only people with this frustrating dilemma; knitters are also faced with it. But once a Personal Pattern is established **EVERY** garment has the potential of fitting correctly.

TIGHT UNDERARM

Do wrinkles occur horizontally across the cap of the sleeve even though it seems roomy enough? Is there also pull across the shoulder blades?

Again we show an illustration of the average body in Fig. I,16b, and an illustration of the body that would experience this problem in Fig. I,16c. Notice the wider back and forward shoulder posture--the pattern must be made to reflect these features. Therefore, more fabric is needed across the back of the bodice and less across the front--it is the proportioning of the bodice that needs altering and **not the sleeve**.

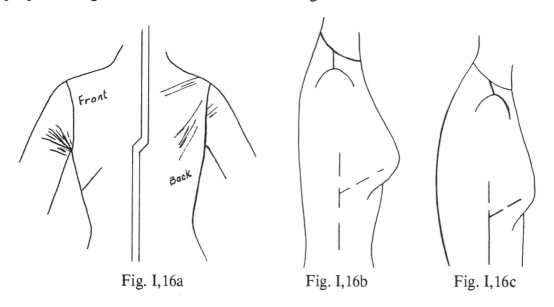

| Fig. I,16a | Fig. I,16b | Fig. I,16c |

To correct, move the shoulder and underarm seams forward.

FRONT

1. Lower the shoulder tip 1/2" *(1.2cm)* more or less and redraw the shoulder line tapering to the existing side neck.

2. Move the front armscye point at least 1/2" *(1.2cm)* inward; redraw the side seam by pinning the dart closed and placing a ruler to connect the waistline to the armscye point.

3. Redraw the front armhole curve the same distance forward of the notch, tapering the line up to the shoulder and out to the armscye point. (See Fig. I,16d.)

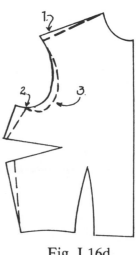

Fig. I,16d

BACK

4. Raise shoulder tip the same distance as the front was lowered and redraw the shoulder line by pinning the shoulder dart closed and tapering the line up to the existing side neck.

5. Move the armhole underarm point the same distance as for the front, making it wider, and taper the line down to the waistline as shown in Fig. I,16e.

6. Redraw curve of back armhole the same distance as for the front outside the notches tapering upward to the shoulder line and downward to the armscye point.

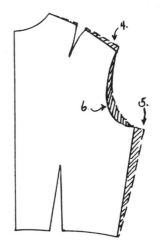

Fig. I,16e

SLEEVE

7. Move the shoulder line joining dot forward the same distance as the back shoulder was raised. (See Fig. I,16f)

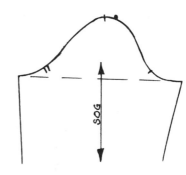

Fig. I,16f

SLEEVES TOO TIGHT

This problem as illustrated by Fig. I,17a may
be caused by any number of situations:

- The measurement was taken too tightly.
- The recommended ease was not
  properly applied.
- The body may have put on more flesh
  since the measurments were taken.

Fig. I,17a

Whatever the cause, it is easily adjusted. Simply determine the amount of additional
room that is needed, divide by two, and add the result to each side seam at the armscye
(base line) and taper down to the wrist. The cap base line will be raised and the cap will
become flatter.

As an example, if an additional 1" *(2.5cm)* of
room is desired, add 1/2" *(1.2cm)* to each side
of the pattern at the cap Base Line and taper
downward to the wrist. Raise the cap Base
Line about 3/4" *(2cm)* and remeasure the cap
to be sure the amount of ease remains the
same (adjusting the cap Base Line upward or
downward to achieve this). Re-draw the cap as
shown in Fig. I,17b, tapering gradually into
the crown area.

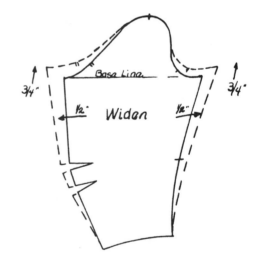

Fig. I,17b

NOTE: The enlarged diagram of the cap in Fig. I,17c illustrates how the adjustment is
accurately drawn. The back tapers into the cap nearer the crown to allow sufficient
forward reach. To prevent excessive bulk (or bubbling), the front should not taper as
high into the crown.

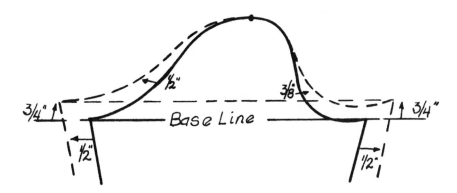

Fig. I,17c

There are several advantages to this technique as opposed to the slash-and-spread method that you may also like:

- The pattern length from shoulder to wrist is not disturbed.
- The cap shaping is more accurately controlled.
- There is no need for sticky tape; therefore it cannot stick where it is not wanted.

GAPPING NECKLINES

Gapping neckline problems have several causes. However, let us assume that fabric handling and sewing ability are not the reasons.

Gapping of a jewel neck is uncomfortable; of a deeper neckline, it could be embarrassing. If the shoulders tend to be pitched forward or if the chest is flat (or hollow), the neckline on almost all commercial patterns will gap as illustrated in Figs. I,18a and 18b.

Some major brand patterns are proportioned with the same shoulder-tip to shoulder-tip measurement across the front as across the back. This may explain why many people (especially women) experience the gapping neckline problem. However, in analyzing the patterns from Burda Pattern Co. we found that the proportioning was different. The back shoulder tip measurement is 1" *(2.5cm)* wider than the front, which is better balance for the female figure and helps to control this fitting problem.

There are bodies, however, that vary much more than 1", even 2 1/2" to 3" *(6.2cm to 7.5cm)*. Then, in addition to changing the front pattern, it may be necessary to also adjust the back as explained in "Sleeve Cap Wrinkles".

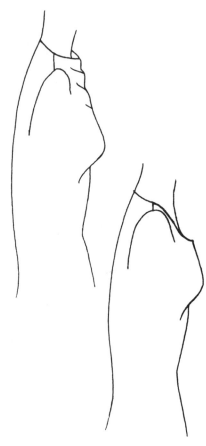

Fig. I,18a and b

To correct the muslin:

1. Rip the stitching along the shoulder seam.

2. Rip the stitching along the front sleeve cap from the shoulder seam to the notch.

3. Smooth the fabric across the front chest. Pin and baste the shoulder seam to desired fit. (The neckline front and back will show a jog.)

4. Mark the muslin with the desired sewing lines at the armscye and trim away the excess fabric.

5. Restitch the front sleeve.

Mark the corrections onto the pattern. They
will look about like the illustration in
Fig. I,18c.

Notice that the same amount taken off the
shoulder is added to the side of the neck. I
refer to this technique as "slipping the seam."
It results in the shoulder-tip to shoulder-tip
between front and back being in proper
balance; fitting smoothly across the upper
chest and neck area of the body for which it
is intended.

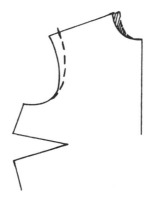

Fig. I,18c

LESSON IN DRAPING

Can you see where it is possible to accentuate
the gapping neckline and call it a "cowl" or
"draped neckline?"

This is accomplished by closing the bust dart
entirely (or partially) and pivoting the
pattern on the Apex. Duplicate the armhole
shape and the length of the shoulder line.
Draw the neckline to your design ideas,
selecting either of the two shown in
Fig. I,18d: a.) curving, or b.) making a
straight line.

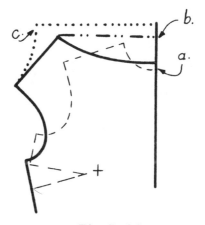

If more drape is desired, widen the distance
between the front shoulder tips and for less
drape, narrow the distance.

Fig. I,18d

To make an even lower front drape, c.) curve the shoulder line upward toward the neck
and draw the neckline at right angles to the Center Front.

UNEVEN NECKLINE

A drag line (or stress line) as shown in Fig. I,19a may occur when the neck is off center. It is more noticeable on a jewel neck garment. The drag line usually disappears on a garment with a scoop neckline, however, the neck appears to be off center in the neck opening, which, of course, it is.

This is quite common, especially for the sports active person such as a swimmer, golfer, tennis player, bowler, etc. A muscle may develop at the base of the back neck between the nape and the shoulder blade of the most-used arm and may even push the spine to one side. Of course, there may be other causes such as arthritis or bursitis, etc.

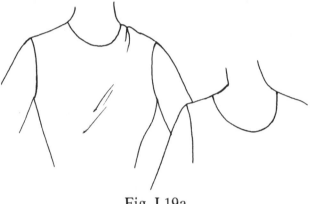

Fig. I,19a

Whatever the cause, the result is that the shoulders can be different widths.

For future designing and all phases of your wardrobe plans, adjusting for this figure trait is recommended. To do so, make a whole pattern with the adjustments for both the left and the right sides.

To correct the muslin:

1. Rip the stitching along the shoulder seam of the side with the stress lines, about 2" *(5cm)* out from the neck.

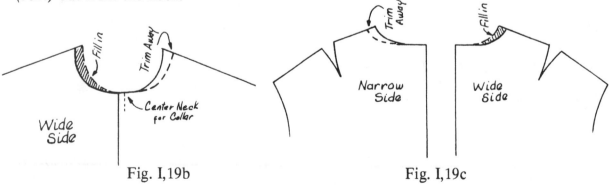

Fig. I,19b   Fig. I,19c

2. Gently tug downward at the waistline allowing the test shell to settle on your body. Mark the muslin for the adjusted neckline on the narrow shoulder side of front and back and trim away the excess. (See Fig. I,19b for Front and Fig. I,19c for Back.)

3. Pin a strip of muslin under the other side of neck to fill in the gap. Draw the desired neckline for this wider shoulder. One shoulder on the pattern is now longer than the other.

If the adjustment is 1/2" *(1.2cm)* or more this will influence the choice of neck design for future styling. The object will be to camouflage the problem--purposely styling asymmetric necklines.

Here are three choices for a neckline opening:

- Make a collar/tie long enough to wrap around the neck and tie off-center to the chin.
- Make an oriental type opening using the mandarin collar; the opening curves across the chest from the center of the neck to the left side seam ending 1-1/2" *(3.7cm)* below the armpit. A zipper at the side extends to the hipline to provide an opening.
- Use a back neck opening. Wear a large square scarf--tying it at the side neck and draping the free corners on the opposite shoulder.

GAPPING ARMHOLES

Gapping armholes usually occur on a person with a more rounded back, prominent shoulder blades (wings), or shoulders that pitch forward. We frequently see this problem on a pattern that has no shoulder dart. Figure I,20a illustrates the possible posture that accompanies this problem.

The dart at the shoulder needs adjusting and the fabric at the shoulder tip will be lifted out.

To correct the muslin:

1. Rip the stitching along the shoulder seam from the shoulder tip to just past the dart; if no dart exists, then rip just past the center of the shoulder seam.

Fig. I,20a

2. Rip the stitching of the dart and press out the creases of the stitching lines.

3. With the muslin on, pin in a wider dart. Lay the front shoulder onto the back and pin in place for the desired fit; reducing the gap but not eliminating all of it. The front will overlap the back shoulder seam at the shoulder tip about 1/2" *(1.2cm)* tapering to the dart. Mark the muslin and make the corrections on the pattern. It will look about like Fig. I,20b. The broken line is the correction. Notice the illustration has an adjustment at the center back line--an additional remedy for correcting this problem.

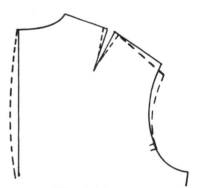

Fig. I,20b

If a seam down the centerback is undesirable, another option is to widen the centerback on the fold about 3/8" to 1/2" *(1cm to 1.2cm)* and add a small dart at the neckline. (See Fig. I,20c.)

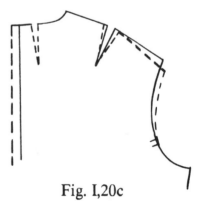

Fig. I,20c

SQUARED SHOULDERS

Do wrinkle lines occur across the upper back, (indicating stress across the neck front and back) extending out to the shoulder tip? Does the neckline seem too big? The initial inclination is to remove the excess fabric at the side neck tapering out to the shoulder tip. (See Fig. I,21b below.)

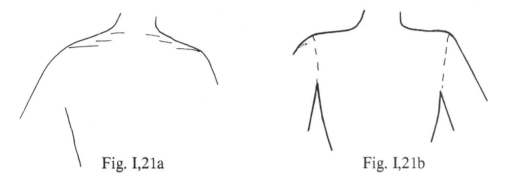

Fig. I,21a   Fig. I,21b

The body with this problem has more squared shoulders than the average slope on the commercial patterns. It may look similar to the one in Fig. I,21b above.

To correct the muslin:

1. Rip the stitching along the shoulder seam, but allow the neck to remain attached.

2. Pull the muslin down until the wrinkles disappear. A space will open along the shoulder line. Lay a strip of fabric under this space and pin the front and back bodice to it.

3. Mark the new shoulder line, dividing the space equally between back and front.

4. Raise the underarm the same amount that is added to the top of the shoulder by re-drawing the armscye.

The shaded areas in Fig. I,21c indicate the correction.

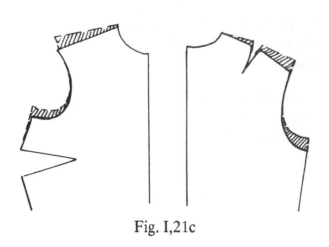

Fig. I,21c

SLOPED SHOULDERS

Do wrinkle lines (drag lines) form from under the armhole and point upward toward the shoulder area? It may or may not look as dramatic as the illustration in Fig. I,22a.

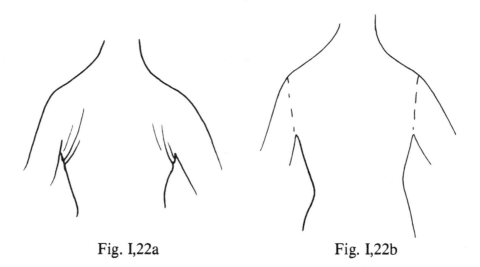

Fig. I,22a   Fig. I,22b

The body that experiences this kind of mis-fitting has shoulders that slope more than the average and may look about like the one in Fig. I,22b.

To correct the muslin:

1. Rip the stitching along the side seam down to the waistline.

2. Pull up the muslin at the shoulder tip until the fabric lies smoothly against the body. Mark the adjusted shoulder seam.

3. Lower the armhole the same amount that is used in lowering the shoulder tip. (See Fig. I,22c.)

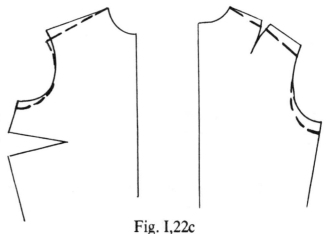

Fig. I,22c

UNEVEN HEMLINE

Does the skirt stick out at one side? Do the centerfront and centerback seams appear to be pulled to one side? This problem is often accompanied by wrinkles on one side of the bodice between the waistline and the armpit. Does Fig. I,23a look like a familiar fitting problem?

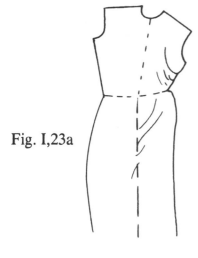

Fig. I,23a

An uneven hemline should almost always be adjusted at the waistline. There are exceptions, however, as in straightening the hemline of a circular skirt. In the latter you would be dealing with fabric variables--sagging in the bias and off-grain areas.

To correct the muslin:

1. Rip the stitching from the waistline seam across the higher side. Allow the lower hip to remain connected to the waistline about 2" *(5cm)* to each side of the side seam.

2. Rip the stitching from the skirt darts and iron out the creases of the side seam sewing line.

3. Baste a strip of fabric across the top of the high side on the skirt.

With the muslin on, loosely tie a string or narrow elastic around the waistline. Pull the skirt into correct appearance with, a.) side seams hanging straight downward, b.) center front and center back hanging straight downward, and c.) hemline as level as possible.

Mark along the stringline the proposed adjusted waistline and pin in the shaping and positioning for the skirt darts. The adjustments may look about like the ones in Fig. I,23b.

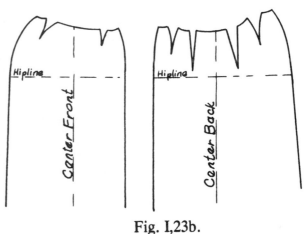

Fig. I,23b.

Quite often it is necessary for darts to be of differing sizes, lengths, and widths as shown in Fig. I,23b. This illustration tells me that one side of the buttocks on this person is larger than the other. In this instance, as in the uneven necklines, a whole pattern should be made. Accuracy built into your pattern now means being able to predict the outcome of fit for whatever style you design--FOREVER!

Whenever the skirt waistline is altered, the bodice needs adjustment as well. It may look like the corrections in Fig. I,23c.

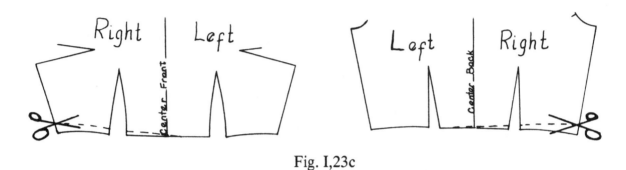

Fig. I,23c

IMPORTANT: The whole pattern should be drawn so that the marked side corresponds to the left and right sides of the body when the pattern is held against you; the marked side on the outside. Use red to indicate Left and green to indicate Right.

FORWARD SIDE SEAMS

Does the skirt stick out in front and the side seams swing forward? Are there also drag (stress) lines extending from the sides upward toward the tummy? (See Fig. I,24a.)

This problem is caused by the pattern having a level waistline while the body, as seen in Fig. I,24b, has a waistline that is high in front and low in back. Part of the cause for the stress lines may be a larger buttocks. Some of that can be corrected by having the appropriately sized main dart on the back pattern. (See DARTS in the Appendix.)

Fig. I,24a

Fig. I,24b

To correct the muslin:

1. Rip the stitching from waistline seam across the front from one side to the other. You may also need to rip along the back waistline.

2. Rip the stitching from the front darts and press out the sewing creases.

3. Baste a 2" *(5cm)* strip of muslin to the front waistline.

4. With the muslin on, pull the skirt front down until the side seams hang straight. Pin the darts to desired fit. Pin the bodice onto the skirt at the adjusted waistline. The shaded area on Fig. I,24c shows the probable changes.

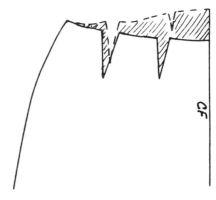

Fig. I,24c

It may or may not be necessary to adjust the bodice waistline. This should be determined before the skirt is reattached to it. (See Fig. I,24d.)

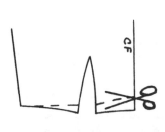

Fig. I,24d

Occasionally altering is needed for those who are higher at the back waistline rather than the front. The same technique is applied--raising the back instead of the front.

NOTE: The bodice darts DO NOT have to line up with the skirt darts. Those on the skirt are positioned for fitting the lower body's curves; likewise, those on the bodice are positioned for fitting the curves of the upper torso. Whether or not they match at the waistline is unimportant.

I have recently added another lady to my "special" list. Lillian is a lovely woman and a pleasure to work with. But because of an unfortunate accident in her youth, her body is not symmetric. In fact one hip is 3" *(7.5cm)* higher than the other. Since she doesn't sew she has had to depend upon others to alter her clothes. One (so called) dressmaker merely leveled the hem of an A-line skirt because, of course, the hem was 3" higher on one side. Because she failed to perform her art properly, the skirt lies flat against the low side and hangs with a large draping fold on the other side. The hemline should have been leveled from the waistline!!

Now that Lillian has a Personal Pattern, anyone can sew for her--even the uneducated person who hemmed her skirt!!

TRYING TO LOSE OR GAIN?

Are you wondering how the pattern will fit when you lose weight? Each of us loses different amounts in different places; rarely does anyone reduce evenly all over. Your clothes will tell you where to make the changes. If you lose 5 to 10 pounds, you can generally take in the side seams. As you lose more, you should consider making the changes to your pattern as noted in the following illustrations.

1. Take the excess off evenly at the center front of the skirt, from waistline to hemline. The darts would not be affected enough to bother moving them outward; but it is something that you should consider anyway. (See Fig. I,25; broken line is the correction.)

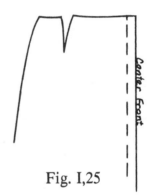

Fig. I,25

2. Make a wider dart on the bodice (under the bust) so the bodice waistline will be equal to that of the skirt. The broken line is the correction. (See Fig. I,26.)

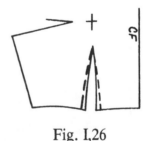

Fig. I,26

As the abdomen is reduced in size, the waistline can be expected to become lower.

3. Note the broken line in Fig. I,27a and 27b; trim off the top of the skirt and add to the lower edge of the bodice.

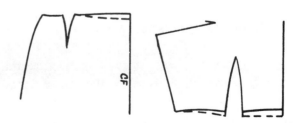

Fig. I,27a and b

For adjustments after gaining weight, simply reverse the process shown in the preceding illustrations:

- Add to the center front of the skirt and
- Lessen the width of the dart under the bust.
- Raise the front waistline on both the skirt and bodice.

If the bosom has increased in size, it may be necessary to make the side bust dart wider and add more length to the front bodice.

For Major Weight Loss:

If there is a greater loss of weight (e.g. over 25 pounds), it could affect the proportioning of the entire upper torso. The illustrations below show some possible adjustments: taking out a small amount across the back at the underarm and at the armscye (Fig. I,28a); taking in a small amount along the front underarm seam, and, at the armscye, making the side bust dart narrower and moving the apex closer to the center front; and trimming length from the waistline (Fig. I,28b). Adjustment to the sleeve will also be needed as shown in Fig. I,28c. (The broken line is the correction.)

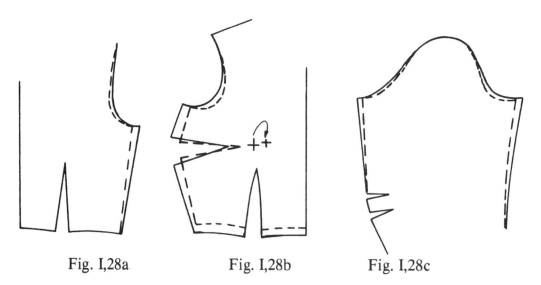

Fig. I,28a   Fig. I,28b   Fig. I,28c

For Major Weight Gain:

If there is a major weight gain, the bodice may need to be expanded to accommodate the larger bosom. Simply reverse the above procedure.

For more detailed instruction on how to change the bust darts, see "Adjusting for the Growing Body" in this chapter.

You could be thinking right about now that it would be easier to start all over again rather than to do these alteration. There's really no need to begin again because the alterations are superficial a.) the bone structure does not change, i.e., shoulder width, arm length, shoulder slope, back neck to waist, and posture that includes the pitch of the shoulder or the upright set of the neck and head, b.) flesh is fairly easy to accommodate compared to bone structure and proportioning--usually there is little or no change to the back. For illustration of sleeve and front bodice adjustment, see Figs. I,29a and 29b below.

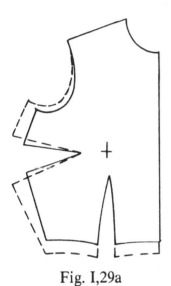

Fig. I,29a

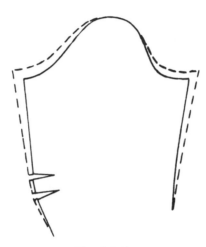

Fig. I,29b

NEVER, BUT NEVER!

Don't ever take in or let out the bodice along the center back or center front!!! This destroys the pattern proportioning and fit of the neckline, collar, shoulder, and armhole!!!

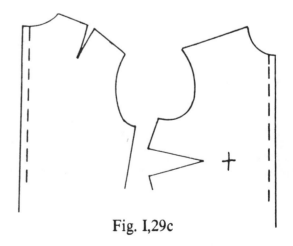

Fig. I,29c

This is wrong!

FLUCTUATING FIGURES

Most of us have days when we feel and look bloated. Some of us have those days more often than we like to. And as the years creep in on us, the muscles do not hold the tummy as flat and trim as they used to. We need to design for these days too and have a few garments ready that will camouflage this problem.

Some bodies fluctuate 5 to 15 pounds in a matter of one to three days. This limits a woman in her garment selection during "that time of the month." The Shift or A-Line styling could be the answer and be more comfortable during this time period; particularly if it is made of any of the knitted fabrics. The softness of jersey adds a more feminine appearance and drapes very nicely when it is allowed to float on the hips and is gently gathered at the waist with a soft belt.

Styles to avoid:

Bias skirts (especially if the fabric is such that a skirt cut on the bias may "cup" in under the bulging tummy). An example of fabric that would be prone to this characteristic is light-weight crepe in any fiber blend. All fabric types considered more appropriate to cut on the bias are gabardine, flannel (if tightly woven), tissue silk, organdy, etc.

What causes "cupping" under the abdomen or buttocks? One cause is the weight of the material pulling against the criss-cross grain; the looser woven fabrics will mold around everything it lays against.

Another cause is that darts, gathers or easing were not handled correctly. For example, a bias skirt for a body with a protruding tummy should be cut large enough from side-to-side to allow ample flare. And the waistline of the skirt must be eased or slightly gathered onto the waistband with **most of the ease centered over the center of the tummy bulge** giving an even distribution to the flaring. (Stretching across the center of the abdomen bulge causes the undesirable cupping.)

If you have a skirt that hangs poorly as described, here is a way to correct the problem:

Remove the waistband, take out the hem, recut the waistline about 1-1/2" to 2" *(3.7cm to 5cm)* lower. After resetting the waistband (remembering to arrange for more of the easing directly above the abdomen) have someone pin and level the hemline while you have it on.

SET A SLEEVE

The "tattle tales" of a home-made garment are the collars and sleeves. They reveal your ability or inexperience as no other place on your garment will.

On woven fabrics especially, it is wise not to shortcut the sleeve setting method!! Whether with set-in or raglan sleeves, the armhole seam must be sewn so that the stitching direction is front to back as opposed to the shortcut methods wherein the side seam of the garment and the underarm seam of the sleeve are sewn in one continuous stitching. This latter method creates wrinkles and puckers in the armpit (more noticeable when the conventional 5/8" *(1.6cm)* seam allowance is used). However, because many knit styles may be sewn together using a very small seam allowance of 1/4" (more or less) *(.6cm)*, the seam direction is a matter of choice and convenience to the sewer.

Is there too much ease in the commercially made patterns so that the sleeve cap cannot fit nicely into the armhole? Many people think so! It depends upon the pattern you are using (see "Inter-Brand Analysis", CHOOSING A PATTERN.) Some of the commercial pattern manufacturers make the sleeve cap ease as much as 2-1/2" *(6.2cm)* or as little as 1" *(2.5cm)*. And one pattern manufacturer actually showed a lesser amount on the sleeve cap than on the bodice armhole. This, of course, is wrong! Quite a variation, isn't it?

It is difficult enough to stitch the convex curve of the sleeve cap into the concave curve of the bodice. (See Fig. I,30a and 30b.) To this, add the standard 5/8" *(1.6cm)* or wider seam allowance and you will experience even greater difficulty. For instance, 1-5/8" *(4cm)* ease is too much when sewing with fabrics such as corduroy, real or imitation leathers, permanent press, some woven linen types, and gabardines; for these I recommend 3/4" to 1" *(2cm to 2.5cm)* of ease. In general, 1-1/8" to 1-1/2" *(2.8cm to 3.7cm)* ease is best for all other fabrics. The lesser ease amount is used on the shorter armhole depth of the more petite (and usually shorter, under 5'2") figure. The greater ease amount is used on the deeper armhole depth of the larger (and generally taller, perhaps over 5'8") figure. See "Restricted Reach," in this chapter, for more detailed information about armhole/sleeve related problems.

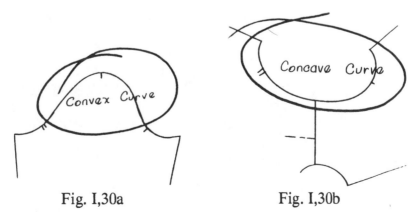

Fig. I,30a   Fig. I,30b

DEFINITION OF A WELL-SET SLEEVE

The machine stitching is not too tight:

Stitches should not break when the armhole is stretched. That does not mean that several rows are needed to keep the armhole from stretching. Unless a flat-fell type seam or a french seam is called for, *only one row of stitching* should be used because repeated stitching will cause puckers along the seam line and make the armhole even smaller and therefore tighter.

The notches on the cap match the notches in the armhole:

There should be *no* easing of the cap in the armpit between the notches. Easing along the crown must be distributed uniformly to avoid puckers and dimples.

Proper width of seams:

Overly wide seam allowances will interfere with good fit in the armpit area especially. If you are waiting to see how it fits before trimming the seam down to 3/8" *(1cm),* **DON'T.** Plunge in--trim away the excess seam--that may be the very reason for the ill fitting sleeve.

The sleeve is set in the circular method:

You may surely expect wrinkles in the armpit area if the circular method is not used. When the side seam of the garment is sewn across the armhole seam and from waist to wrist in one operation that is called the flat method. Use of this method should be limited in application where 1/4" *(.6cm)* seams (or less) are suitable as on sweater type construction.

The excessive ease found in commercial patterns is not present in a personal pattern. Setting sleeves will never again be a problem if you follow these few simple suggestions:

1. Maintain a maximum seam allowance of 3/8" *(1cm)* at the armscye and the sleeve cap. The wider the seam allowance, the greater the difficulty in handling the ease.

2. Contain the ease within the cap, above the notches and as much into the crown area as possible. Especially important is keeping the front sleeve ease well into the crown and not along the forward (mid-chest) area.

The ease stitching is confined to an area from about 2" *(5cm)* forward of the notch at the crown to the notches at the back.

3. Reduce the amount of ease only when designing for the tightly woven or hard-finished materials such as suede types, corduroy, permanent press, twill, gabardine, etc.

Check the sleeve cap ease before setting it into the garment. Stand a tape on edge and measure the sewing line of the armscye on the garment and the cap of the sleeve as shown in Fig. I,31. The sleeve measurement should be 1-1/8" to 1-1/2" *(2.8cm to 3.7cm)* longer. However, if ease is to be reduced a small amount, it may be done by the following procedure:

To reduce the ease by approximately 1/2" *(1.2cm)*, draw a line horizontally across the cap midway between the Base Line and the Crown. Draw another line parallel to the first so that the lines are 1/4" *(.6cm)* apart. Fold out the ease by joining these two lines as shown in Fig. I,32a. Redraw the sides of the cap to make a smooth line; note the broken line as illustrated in the enlargement which is Fig. I,32b.

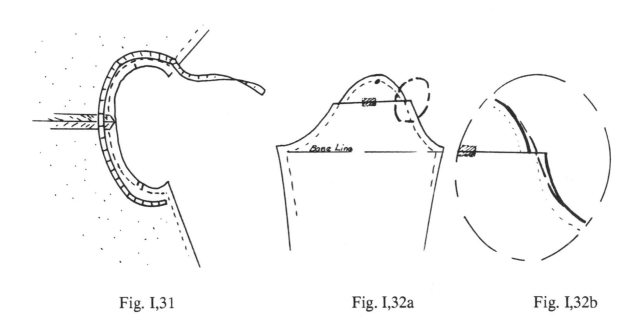

Fig. I,31   Fig. I,32a   Fig. I,32b

SEWING SEQUENCE

The following method was developed and used in my factory over 25 years ago. It is a combination of the flat and conventional (circular) construction methods.

First, use only a 3/8" *(1cm)* seam allowance on the armscye of the body and the cap of the sleeve.

1. Stitch the shoulder seams of the garment and press them open. Do not stitch the side seams until step 7. Measure the stitching line by placing a tape measure on its edge as shown in Fig. I,33. If the fabric tends to stretch, it may not be possible to get an accurate reading; then measure the pattern piece instead.

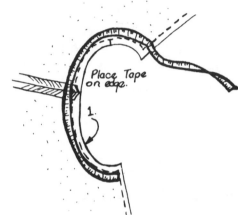

Fig. I,33

2. Using about 8 stitches per inch *(2.5cm)* make two rows of stitching within the seam allowance about 1/4" *(.6cm)* apart. Stitch around the cap of the sleeve between the notches with the first row either on the sewing line or just inside it. (See step 2 in Fig. I,34.)

3. Pull up the stitching from both ends until the sleeve cap stitching line measures the same as the armscye line.

Fig. I,34

4. Now use the smaller end of dressmaker's ham, which is about the shape of the top of your shoulder. Stand the ham on the broader end in front of you. Pin the center of the crown of the sleeve to the top center of the ham with the face of the fabric against the face of the ham. Fit the cap over the edge of the ham as far as the notches and pin to secure. Distribute the fullness evenly and gently press in the fullness. (See Fig. I,35.)

Fig. I,35

5. Pin sleeve to bodice, matching the notches and shoulder seam to the larger dot at the crown. (See step 5, Fig. I,36.)

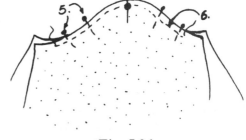

Fig. I,36

6. With bodice *under* the sleeve, begin stitching 1-1/2" *(3.7cm)* in from the underarm seam, around the cap to within 1-1/2" of the other underarm seam. (See Fig. I,36.) Remove pins. (A light touch of pressing may be desirable at this point while the garment is open and easy to handle over the ham). Lay seam allowances into the sleeve.

7. Stitch sleeve underarm seams together from armpit to wrist. Stitch bodice side seams together beginning at armscye. (See step 7, Fig. I,37 noting the direction of arrows.)

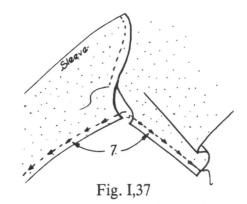

Fig. I,37

8. Turn sleeve and drop it inside the bodice. Complete sewing in the sleeve, overlapping the stitching lines about 1/2" *(1.2cm)*. (See step 8 in Fig. I,38.) Remove all easing stitches.

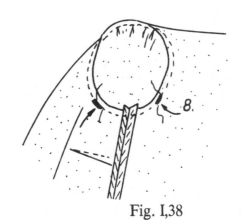

Fig. I,38

SETTING A SLEEVE WAS NEVER EASIER!!

THE MASTER PATTERN

PROOFING THE DRAFT

After completing the alterations of the test garment and adjustments on the pattern, it is important to "proof" the pattern. The lengths and shaping of the seams that will be joined together must match. The curves at the shoulder tip, neckline, armpit, waistline, and sleeve cap must blend together smoothly without peaks or valleys.

BODICE

1. **Proof the Shoulder/Armscye Curve.** (See Fig. I,39.) Place the shoulder lines of the Back and Front bodice parts together at the shoulder tip. This prevents a potential distortion of the sleeve cap. Make a notch where the back shoulder dart joins the Front Bodice.

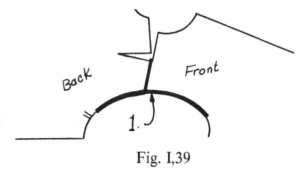

Fig. I,39

2. **Proof the Neckline Curve.** (See Fig. I,40.) Join shoulder seam at the neck edge; refine the curve and apply neck measurement. Make the neckline larger or smaller as necessary.

3. **Verify.** Remember that the Centerfront and Centerback neckline is squared. (See Fig. I,40.) This will also help prevent peaks or valleys when the pattern is laid on the folded fabric.

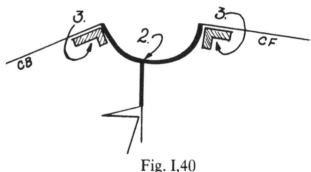

Fig. I,40

4. **Proof Armpit Curve.** Place underarm seams together at the armscye points. This will equalize the strain to the underarm seam and prevent stress that may rupture the stitching. Smooth, gentle curves are stronger and can take more strain. (See Fig. I,41.) Make a notch where the bust dart joins the back bodice.

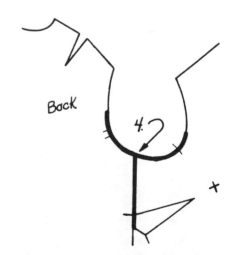

Fig. I,41

5. **Proof Side Seam Lengths.** Place underarm seams of Back and Front bodice together between the bust dart and the waistline. (See Fig. I,42a.)

6. **Verify** that the Centerfront and Centerback waistlines are squared. This will prevent peaks and valleys when cutting on the fold. (See Fig. I,42a "back" and Fig. I,42b "front.")

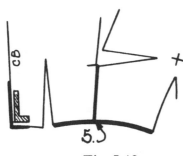

Fig. I,42a

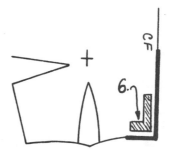

Fig. I,42b

SLEEVE

7. **Proof Cap Base Line Curves.** (See Fig. I,43.) Join the underarm seams; place them together along the SOG line on the center of the sleeve. Draw a smooth curve along the armpit area. Indicate place where elbow darts join to front arm seam.

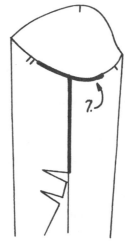

Fig. I,43

SKIRT

8. **Verify** that the Centerfront and Centerback waistline and the hemline are squared. (See Fig. I,44.)

9. **Proof Side Seam Lengths.** Join the skirt parts at the side seam. Use a straight ruler or a curve stick to make a smooth hemline.

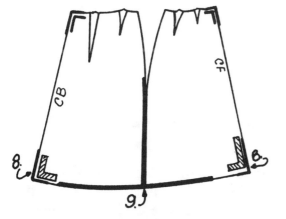

Fig. I,44

MAKE A MASTER PATTERN

The way is now open to the most enjoyable sewing you have ever experienced. Whether you use your sloper to adjust the mass produced patterns or to create original designs, you will find it to be the most valuable sewing tool you ever owned.

There are several ways to make a permanent pattern.
- Transfer the master pattern to a medium-weight, non-woven, semi-stiff interfacing material (such as Pellon® #40). It is easy to work with, washable, and will keep its shape and newness after many, many years of steady use. (This is the method I prefer and recommend in my classes.) It is explained in four easy steps below.
- Reproduce the master pattern on cardboard; a stripped pattern--without seam allowances. Cut a round hole near a corner and hang it by a string threaded through the hole. (Most of the garment factories store their master patterns in this manner.)
- Redraw your final draft onto paper and reinforce the paper by ironing one of the fusible interfacing materials onto the reverse side. (I have become disenchanted with this method because after a relatively short period of time, the paper becomes torn and pulls away from the interfacing material.)

To Transfer the Master Pattern to PELLON®

1. Lay the adjusted pattern onto a sheet of white paper. Place the Pellon on top and pin all layers together to keep them from slipping. The lines of the pattern can easily be seen through the #40 Pellon® because of the white paper beneath. (See Fig. I,45.)

2. Draw onto the Pellon®; using fine line felt tip pens or colored pencils to trace all the sewing lines, darts, hiplines, apex, and hemlines, etc. The rulers and curves will assist in making accurate, neat lines.

Fig. I,45

3. As shown in Fig. I,45, leave plenty of margin around the perimeter of the sewing lines; it is useful for notations and fitting revisions. (If you cut out the pattern along the sewing lines, you will find them more difficult to trace; the cut edge tends to curl and

push away from the tracing wheel. An exception is when the pattern is made in cardboard.)

4. Do not add seam allowances to these pattern parts because, like in a factory, you will be working with a stripped pattern. As you will see, designing with only the stitching line can be far more accurate--the seam allowances are added **after** the designing of a fashion garment is completed.

The pants pattern will be different, however. Here you may add seam allowances and cut it out--using the pattern itself to lay directly onto the fabric. When cutting, try to be careful and avoid cutting anything off your master pattern each time you use it or the seam allowances could get progressively narrower. It is always advisable to use a tracing wheel with tracing paper to mark the sewing lines accurately--especially for duplicating the crotch curves and darts.

Your master pattern is a permanent record of you. With reasonable care, it will serve you well for the rest of your life. However, suppose that over a period of time, changes take place in your body shape and posture that suggest adjustments are needed. If you have kept the muslin, you can put it on again in a few years and make a few simple adjustments without having to redo the entire process.

When any alteration questions arise, refer to FITTING PROBLEMS AND THEIR CORRECTIONS. It is a valuable source of information that explains in detail the causes of the fitting problems and how to make corrections. Most of these techniques have not been published before now; they are the accumulation of years of experience gained through working with over 7,000 people (on an individual basis). By adding the other titles to your library, you will own a powerful resourse for instant knowledge.

WHAT NOW?

There are so many wonderful ideas in fashion that can be easily copied. Your sloper is the key to an exciting future with knitting as well as with sewing. Even crocheted garments may be made to fit the way you want them to.

In INTRODUCTION TO DESIGN you will be introduced to some simple designing--showing how to make a Shift and a shift-style with French Dart variations in a matter of minutes and still maintain control of the perfect fit that was built into the sloper. You now can make a variety of collars and sleeves in building a collection (a library) of interchangeable pattern parts.

Commercially printed patterns can be accurately adjusted to fit, too! By laying them across a master pattern, the deviation becomes obvious. Keep in mind, however, that the commercial designer may have intended a fashion with a lot of ease as styling detail--so if you want to copy their style, you must be careful not to destroy or eliminate the fashion flare.

Laura is a professional. She has worn a size 8 Vogue for many years. When she completed a blouse (made of very expensive silk) she gave it to her size 12 sister whom it fit beautifully. What a wonderful gift for the sister--however, Laura still needs a silk blouse and (quite frankly) couldn't spare the time or the costly fabric to sew for her sister at this time. What can be done to prevent this situation from recurring?

We'll call this a learning experience for Laura. She now knows that laying the commercial pattern over a blueprint of her body would have instantly shown her what to expect--giving her the opportunity to decide whether to adjust it or accept it as it is.

- -

Most of us have spent many hours fitting other people. When is it our turn to get fitted right? What we all want, of course, is a clone so we can fit IT and, as a result, we can have every garment fit US perfectly. The solution to that dilemma is found in a Personal Pattern--a sloper--that's our clone!!!

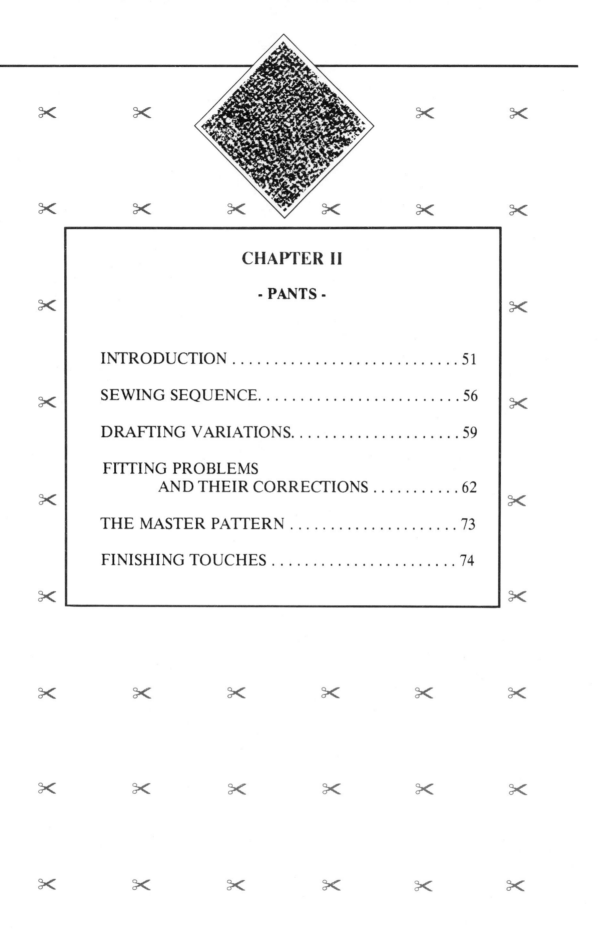

CHAPTER II

- PANTS -

CHAPTER II
--PANTS--

INTRODUCTION

The following characteristics are common and should in no way be considered to be "poor fit." When we understand certain facts, we have an opportunity to modify them; but we may have to compromise instead of fighting circumstances--because there may not be a complete remedy to achieve what you want.

The word pants is a rather general term. Pants come in the form of slacks, jeans, basic pants, trousers, culottes, and shorts.

Pants have basic characteristics of fit that are, at times, questioned by those who are not acquainted with the purpose of these characteristics. It is helpful to remember that pants serve a different function from the one skirts serve, that there are a wide variety of styles for pants because of the broad range of activities for which they are intended. They will all pull down in the back when we sit, unless a.) the crotch depth is lowered or b.) a large enough fold (creating slack) is put under the seat. They all wrinkle across the lap when we sit down--but then, so does a skirt.

With the exception of shorts and culottes, they will all show some pull along the inside of the leg near the crotch when we are walking or sitting. Shorts because of their length, Culottes because their width.

Again, with the exception of shorts and culottes, they will all feel more or less snug across the knees when we sit depending upon the amount of slack under the seat, how slim the legs are, and whether or not we pull the legs up slightly as we sit, which also helps to prevent baggy knees. They will feel very tight if the slack under the buttocks is totally eliminated, not so tight if some is allowed to remain; tighter when the legs of the garment are made slimmer; and tight if we do not lift the pants leg somewhat as we sit--a couple of inches *(4cm to 6cm)* is all that is necessary.

Definition of pants lengths:

    Bermudas - - - - - - just above knee
    Calf Skinners- - - - mid-calf
    Capris - - - - - - - - just below calf
    Jamaicas- - - - - - - mid-thigh
    Pedal Pushers - - - half-way between mid-calf and knee
    Shorts- - - - - - - - - top of thigh
    Slacks- - - - - - - - - ankle length

Shorts may be cut-off version of slacks, jeans, or basic pants.

Culottes may be made with the waistline styling that resembles either basic pants and slacks or a skirt. The variations of styling and usage are seemingly unlimited.

Jeans are a working style where the cut is different from the basic pants or trousers. This particular cut allows more mobility in labor-type activity such as being on a horse, getting on and off machinery, etc.

Slacks and Trousers are made for casual and dressy occasions. The word "trousers" is usually associated with menswear. The type fabric used helps denote the difference between trousers and slacks. The dictionary says:

> Slacks: full cut trousers for casual wear worn
> by men and women.

Pants is the abbreviation of the word "pantaloons." Although the term also may be used for meaning "panties" and "drawers," it is used here to mean the basic pants from which the fashion styling is done. (Making pants on a knitting machine will be covered in KNITTING TO YOUR BASIC PATTERN -- a publication to be released in 1987.)

PERFECT FIT FOR ALL!

Pants have become an acceptable standard of dress for all bodies large or small, male or female, and they canbe made to fit ANY body. Helping you to understand the pattern requirements for each particular shape and posture is why this book is written.

Remember: The pattern should reflect all the shaping that the wearer's body requires if it is to be a true blueprint.

1. All darts shaped to each body's needs to including adding darts rather than making existing darts wider (which may not fit smoothly across the curves).

2. The inseam slanted, straightened, or curved to accommodate any bone/flesh configuration.

3. Crotch seams can be very uncomfortable if not curved to duplicate each body's pelvic shape.

4. Address each area of fit, one at a time; write down the OBSERVATIONS--they are as vital information as the measurements.

Measure large enough. The end result of your effort will be admired if the garment fits well. It will be easier for you to adjust the fit and proportioning on a looser muslin than on one that fits too tightly. So measuring too tightly defeats the purpose and obstructs your fitting attempts.

DEFINING GOOD FIT

Three definitions of good fit for basic pants. Since it may not always be possible to achieve the ideal fit, I have defined two additional categories of fit that allow for the compromises necessitated by the variety of shapes and sizes that people come in.

They each may require a different technique in fitting.

THE IDEAL   THE BEST POSSIBLE   THE ACCEPTABLE

THE IDEAL

Standing with feet about 4" *(10cm)* apart, side seams hang perfectly straight down over the sides from the waistline to hemline, without curving under a thigh bulge or emphasyzing it.

Darts are positioned to serve the function for which they are intended. Whether using 4, 6, or 8 darts, each one reflects the shape of the curves at the high hip. If pleats are used instead of darts as on slacks, there is enough ease across the front to eliminate stress lines.

Crease Lines begin at the crotch depth line, usually halfway between the inseam and side seam. The front drops straight down across the center of the knee and just touches the center of the toe on the shoe. The back drops straight down from the crotch depth line to the center of the heel on the shoe, ending about 3/4" *(2cm)* off the floor.

Leg Width in front allows 1/2" *(1.2cm)* or more of ease across the thigh area--the shape of the body's leg should not be visible.

Crotch fit in front does not reveal the shape of the pelvic area. Nor does the shape of the inseam produce a keyhole effect near the crotch. (Use care in pressing! See "Finishing Touches".)

Seat shaping will gently curve under the seat and not necessarily hang straight as a skirt does. A small fold is often needed to allow for body comfort when in a sitting position. If this fold is eliminated, the waistline will draw down in back and cause the front waistband to press into the stomach which may be uncomfortable.

Center Front seam above the crotch curve is a straight line.

Ease around the main torso is sufficient so that no stress line is produced or that the undergarment lines are unnoticed.

Width of leg at hemline is normally dictated by fashion. However, a good basic rule is for the width to be no wider than the length of the shoe and no narrower than about 1-1/4" *(3.2cm)* back from the point of the shoe.

Hanging on a hanger, it may be folded at the knee or thigh level without distorting the balance of the pants leg and in turn messing the crease lines.

In order to produce such an Ideal garment, the body should have all of the favorable characteristics: the inner side of the knees should not be knobby or touching, the calf of the lower leg would not protrude, there would be no excessive thigh bulges at the outer sides of the leg.

THE BEST POSSIBLE

Side Seams, same as Ideal.

Darts, same as Ideal.

Crease Lines, similar to Ideal except that the front drops straight down regardless of whether it crosses over the center of the knee; and regardless of whether the back hangs at the center of the heel. This variation is necessitated by legs that are bent, i.e., knock kneed.

Leg Width, same as Ideal.

Crotch shaping, same as Ideal; with no keyhole effect.

Seat shaping will be gently curved with a little more fold than Ideal in order to provide sufficient sitting comfort--especially for the body with a larger buttocks. The body that requires this additional attention is illustrated in Fig. II,14i.

Center Front seam above the crotch molds to the body shape regardless of how the pattern looks.

Ease, same as Ideal.

Width of Leg at hemline, same as Ideal. Notice that more width is allowed across the back pattern to accommodate the leg structure illustrated in Fig. II,14a.

Hanging folded over a hanger is not recommended because it usually messes the crease line.

THE ACCEPTABLE

Side Seams may slant backward somewhat toward the foot. It may also be necessary to give more room at the sides for a thigh bulge; showing the thigh bulge somewhat.

Darts are in proper position. In making styles where pleats in front are used the body structure may create undesireable stress on them. When this occurs, it might be more appropriate to substitute slight gathers across the front.

Crease Lines in front hang straight down regardless of the position of the knee beneath. Just because the knees are tight together does not mean the crease line cannot cover up a distracting figure trait. This body type and the pattern adjustment is shown in Fig. II,12c.

Leg width, **Crotch**, and **Ease** are same as Ideal.

Seat Shaping is more pronounced as in The Best Possible.

Width of Leg is same as The Best Possible. Pattern modification may be necessary using the stretch and shrink-shape method.

Hanging by the hemline is the best and only way to store this garment so that the crease lines are not messed. Ask your cleaners to "Dry clean only" (I strongly suggest you do your own pressing for maintaining the correct positioning of the crease line.)

SEWING SEQUENCE

It is very important that the garment seams are sewn accurately. This act, when carefully done, will help you to make the proper adjustments on the pattern.

1. Stitch darts from waistline seam toward the point. DO NOT STITCH INTO THE WAISTLINE SEAM ALLOWANCE; in this manner the seam allowance can be manipulated easily whether a band or a facing is applied. Press the fold toward the center seam.

2. Stitch each leg separately at the inner seam, beginning at the hem edge. (See Fig. II,1.) Use marks at knee as notches for matching. Press seams open.

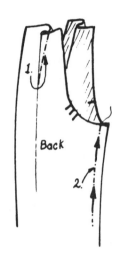

Fig. II,1

It may be necessary to slightly stretch the back inner seam between the knee and crotch to match the front seam length, depending upon how the pattern was drafted. (Refer to "Baggy Seat".)

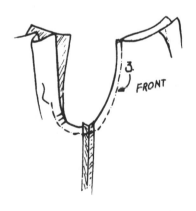

Fig. II,2a

3a. Stitch crotch seam in one continuous sewing line from front to back. (See Fig. II,2a.)

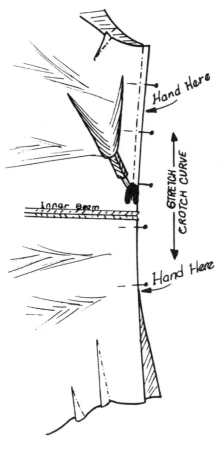

Fig. II,2b

b. Stretch the curve of the crotch as it is run through the machine by holding the fabric with one hand in front of the needle and the other behind, as shown in Fig. II,2b.

c. The trial muslin does not need the second row of sewing. However, a second row will add strength to the crotch area and is recommended for stretchy fabrics. Keep this second row of stitching close to the first, within the seam allowance. (See Fig. II,3.)

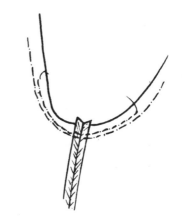

Fig. II,3

4a. Trim the crotch seam, along the curved area, to only 3/8" *(1cm)*. Press open only the straight area of the seam above the curves, front and back. NEVER press open the curve of the crotch seam! Pressing this area open distorts the shape of the surrounding fabric; it is often the cause of the unattractive keyhole effect. (See Fig. II,4.)

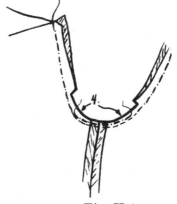

Fig. II,4

b. If the fabric in the seam area needs pressing, it should be pressed closed, over sleeve board as shown in Fig. II,5.

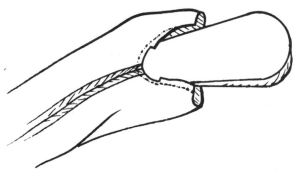

Fig. II,5

NEVER CLIP INTO THE SEAM ALLOWANCE. Clipping weakens the seam and a rip may result (especially on a woven fabric), perhaps at an inappropriate time!

The crotch seam is subjected to the most strain of any seam in our pants and will remain strongest and fit the best by simply trimming the curve smoothly. If necessary, zig-zag or bind the curve to keep the fabric from raveling.

5. Stitch side seams. Stitch from hem to waistline, just as the inner seam was stitched. It makes very little difference to the experienced sewer which direction you stitch; however, you will always have predictable results in the drape of any garment if all the seams are stitched in the same direction. (See Fig. II,6.)

Press the shaped seams open over a ham to maintain their shape.

Fig. II,6

6. Stitch the waistband or facing onto the pant. Have you noticed that the pant waistline is 1" to 1-1/2" *(2.5cm to 3.8cm)* larger than the waistband? This additional amount should be eased onto the band in an area 2" to 4" *(5cm to 10cm)* to each side of the side seams and in front above the tummy; but not across the flat part of the center back.

DRAFTING VARIATIONS

A pants pattern is easy to draw, but how it fits the body for which it is intended depends upon how well the patternmaker did his/her job. That job includes close attention to details such as posture of the body and distribution of muscles and flesh; in other words--appling the observations we make to the pattern.

Since no two of us are exactly alike, there are variations that must be considered and applied to each pattern. And even though more than two people can have the exact same measurements, it does not mean they can wear and look well in each others pants (or other clothing).

Let's look at a few Center Front variations and their side seam counterpart to see how we arrive at the decision for drawing these lines shown in Fig. II,7.

 a. For a flat tummy, small waistline, large thighs. If the body illustrated in Fig. II,14b were to put on a garment from this pattern, there would be stress lines pulling from the tummy outward toward the hips. The fabric across the thighs would not be evenly distributed but would collect to the inner leg just under the crotch.

 b. For a tummy that is more forward for whatever reason (posture, perhaps) as shown in Fig. II,13b.

 c. For a much larger tummy or suitable for a pregnant woman.

Fig. II,7

And a look at some Center Back variations and what they mean.

 a. For the extended seat. If the body illustrated in Fig. II,14i were to put on a garment made from this pattern, there would be a lot of extra fabric under the seat, collected toward the center. This cut is similar to Jean's styling. When combined with "a" (front), it allows the wearer to sit astride a horse without stress on the crotch seams.

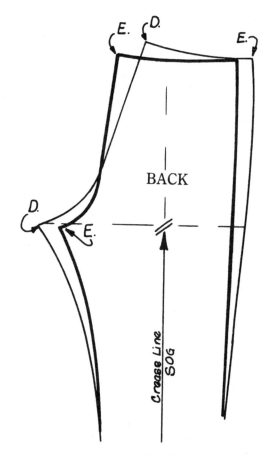

Fig. II,8

b. For the body with a flatter buttocks. Notice that part of the excess fullness is also removed from the sides (Fig. II,8) as indicated by the darker lines.

A correctly shaped crotch curve will provide comfort. It will also appear smooth in the forward pelvic area.

a. The person who feels uncomfortable, as though being cut in two, needs the adjustment illustrated by the broken line in Fig. II,9. A benefit of this procedure is the elimination of pouches that tend to form along the crotch seam because of the protrusion of the pelvic bone or flesh, or the overly slanted crotch curve.

In order to realize the effect of this alteration, the seam must be trimmed to 1/4" *(.6cm)*. It is advisable to adjust this seam in small amounts; even if it takes 3 or 4 times to attain the desired result, trimming out the seam with each change of the stitching line.

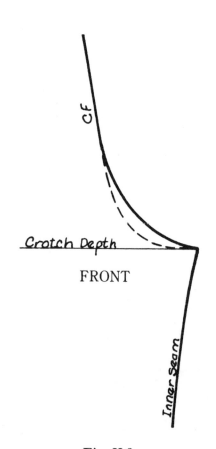

Fig. II,9

b. Correctly applied seat shaping will also produce more comfort. The seam will appear flatter between the cheeks of the buttocks and not feel or look as though it were cutting between them. (See Fig. II.10.)

The person feels uncomfortable because she has a lower (drooping) buttocks and because the crotch curve on the pattern is too slanted. Lower the curve of the seat line about 5/8" *(1.5cm)* below the Crotch Depth line. In this way the back inner seam must be stretched onto the front. (A narrow seam allowance facilitates the stretch.) Notice that the broken line shows a more "J"-like shape compared to the original slanted CB line. Do this adjustment in small amounts at a time. Trim the crotch seam before trying on again.

It may or may not be necessary to adjust the waistline--cutting it down results in the pants being pulled up. This technique is used to eliminate the horizontal fold (excessive slack) under the seat line.

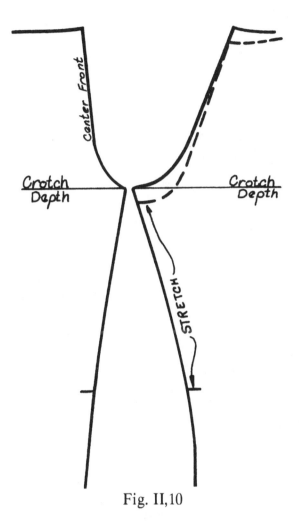

Fig. II,10

How to select a commercial pattern size.

In selecting the correct pattern size, consider the measurement across the back hipline from side seam to side seam.

1. If body measurements show a difference of 1-1/2" to 2" *(3.7cm to 5cm)* between the Hip and the High Hip, buy to fit the Hip measurement.

2. If the difference is no more than 1/4" to 3/4" *(.6cm to 2cm)*, buy a pattern one size larger than the Hip measurement. This small difference indicates a flat buttocks and therefore the only proportion corrections will be to make the back of the pattern smaller. (See Fig. II,14h.)

3. If the difference is 3" to 4" *(7.5cm to 10cm)*, you should buy a pattern one size smaller than the Hip measurement. The difference indicates an extended buttocks and the proportioning corrections will be made to the back pattern only. (See Fig. II,14j.)

FITTING PROBLEMS AND THEIR CORRECTIONS

When a circumstance exists that we cannot handle we call it "a problem," but, with understanding, the problem disappears. So then, *UNDERSTANDING* is the tool that will manipulate an undesirable circumstance into a satisfying solution.

For every wrinkle there could be several causes. Their meaning must be correctly interpreted in order to achieve satisfactory results.

SMILES

SMILES are distinguished by stress lines that originate in the front crotch area and radiate upward toward the waist. In addition, the creasline is pulled inward above the knee.

  a. Crotch seam allowance may be too wide.

CORRECTION: Trim the excess seam allowance from the crotch curve. Do not leave wide seams here thinking it will allow room for correction--wide seams at the sides are acceptable but not in the crotch curve. "There are smiles that make us happy", as the song goes, but not when we see them on pants. (See Fig. II,11a.)

  b. Not enough fabric in Front Thigh area.

This occurs when the Front thigh is very muscular, usually on a more athletic person, or a dancer.

CORRECTION: More fabric is needed across the front thigh area. Extend the front crotch seam the desired width, 5/8" *(1.6cm)* or more, and taper downward to the knee area. Also flatten the crotch curve to eliminate stress across the pelvic area. (See Fig. II,11b.)

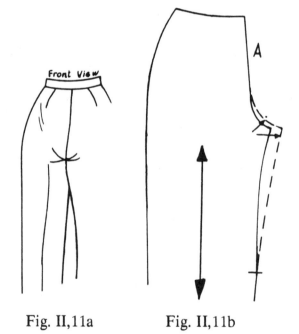

Fig. II,11a   Fig. II,11b

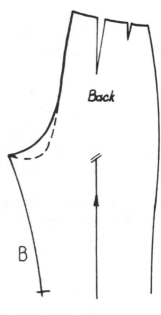

c. Too little fabric across the buttocks. An extended buttocks causes the front to be pulled toward the back; resulting in smiles.

CORRECTION: Cut the back crotch deeper. It may even be necessary to combine this alteration with the correction in "b" if front Creaseline remains distorted. (See Fig. II,11c.)

Fig. II,11c

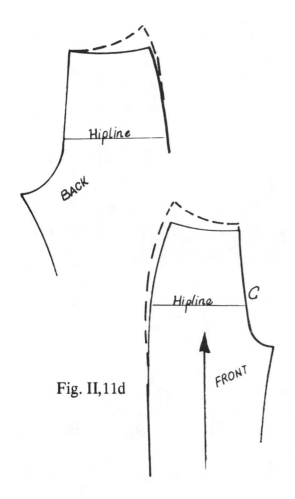

Fig. II,11d

d. Pants are not curved enough at the sides, creating a short crotch effect and smile lines pointing upward to the high waistline.

CORRECTION: Rip the side seams from Waistline to Hipline. Pull the pants down at the sides until the Crotch Depth line is level (or until the smile has disappeared). Measure the space between the top of pants and the body waistline. The corrections to both the front and back patterns could look about like Fig. II,11d. The broken line represents the correction.

SAGS

SAGS are sometimes called smiles by those who are not sure what to call this problem. However, sags usually start lower on the leg. Extra fabric that flaps between the ankles and the creasline, which swings inward at the hemline rather than hanging straight down, characterize this fitting problem. (See Fig. II,12a.)

The pants inseam is too concave for the posture of this body whose knees are touching even when the feet are apart.

CORRECTION: Rip the inseam from Hemline to crotch. Allow fabric and creasline to fall straight down the leg. Straighten the inseam from crotch to hem by filling in the resulting separation. It may or may not be necessary to also shape the crotch deeper into the pants front. And *PLEASE* trim the crotch seam to 1/4" or 3/8" *(.6cm to 1cm)* before trying the pants on. Excessive seam allowances cause all sorts of fitting problems!! The correction is shown by the broken line in Fig. II,12b

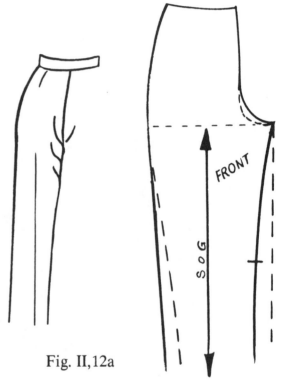

Fig. II,12a

Fig. II,12b

This particular adjustment should be explained in more detail. Most people require at least some degree of this correction. Why? Because there is no pattern made that correctly deals with this fitting problem; including patterns in the garment industry. Let's compare two different body shapes, each standing with feet a few inches apart. (See Fig. II,12c and 12d on next page.)

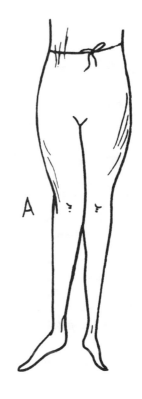

Figure II,12c shows that the knees and inner legs are touching each other in varying degrees of light to firm and in some instances they may even overlap.

Fig. II,12c A

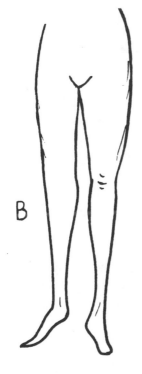

Fig. II,12d B

Figure II,12d shows that the knees and inner legs are separated by at least 1/2" *(1.2cm)*. Most commercial patterns would be acceptable for this body type in but not for the type in Fig. II,12c above.

For some bodies, shaping the inner seam, as shown by the broken line in Fig. II,12e is sufficient. Other bodies may require the adjustment represented by the dash-dot line. Notice that it is drawn with a convex curve between the crotch and the knee to accommodate the distinct posture of the leg. The creaseline placement should be marked by visual means onto the muslin during the fitting; it will not be centered on the pants leg between the inner seam and side seam nor will it be located over the center of the knee cap. Because of this special placement, in order to keep its press from becoming messy, the pants should be hung by the hemline instead of being folded over a hanger. (I recommend the hemline hanging method for all pants.)

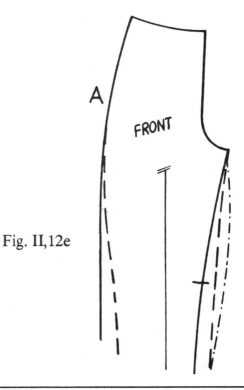

Fig. II,12e

A

FRONT

BULGES

BULGES at the ends of the darts, as shown in Fig. II,13a. Most sewers are inclined to take in these little bulges, extending the dart a few more inches in length. Since they are caused primarily by the darts' being too wide at the waistline, the simpler (more successful) alteration is to make the darts narrower.

Fig. II,13a

Let's look at the profile of three typical bodies and evaluate the accompanying pattern corrections that involve dart shaping and dart width.

 A. The first body type (Fig. II,13b) shows no indentation at the waistline above the tummy.

CORRECTION: Due to the lack of waistline indentation, there is no need for a dart. Perhaps just one dart nearer the side might be appropriate for reducing the fabric between the hip bone and waistline. It should be about 3/8" *(1cm)* wide and about 3" *(7.5cm)* long. (See dart placement in Fig. II,13c.) In addition, the center front seam is made parallel to the SOG line rather than slanted. And notice that the Front waistline is raised to accommodate the high tummy.

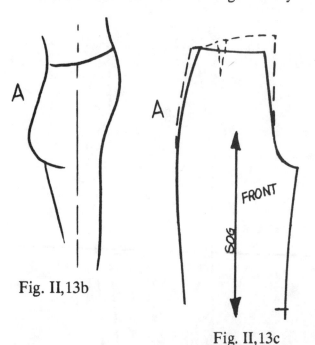

Fig. II,13b

Fig. II,13c

To adjust the garment: Rip the center front seam and the side seams. Re-lay the fabric smoothly against the body and use strips of muslin to fill in the seams that are not meeting. Our goal is to create a pattern that covers the body properly regardless of the unorthodox appearance of the pattern.

The broken line in Fig. II,13c shows how the correction may look in relationship to a purchased pattern (represented here by the solid line).

B. The second body type (Fig. II,13d) has a small waistline, but a more protruding tummy.

CORRECTION: The pattern needs two darts positioned above the tummy to shape the fabric into the waistline. Both darts are convex--the one near the center front might be only 3/8" *(1cm)* wide and 1-1/2" *(3.7cm)* long; the other, near the side seam, should not be over 3" *(7.5cm)* long and 3/8" to 3/4" *(1cm to 2cm)* wide. (See Fig. II,13e.) In addition, the front seam is curved to accommodate the roundness of the tummy and prevent stress lines between it and the side seams. The Front Waistline is raised (drawn in higher than the previous waistline).

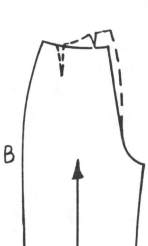

Fig. II,13d

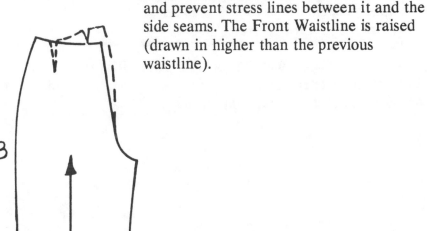

Fig. II,13e

C. The third body type (Fig. II,13f) has a flatter tummy than either of the other two. And because this is probably a more active body, it may have more muscular thighs; and the Center Front is more slanted.

CORRECTION: The only place that will require a dart is the forward hip bone for shaping the fabric into the small waistline--shown in Fig. II,13g.

Fig. II,13f

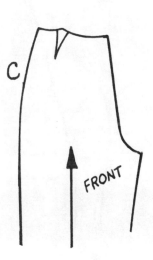

Fig. II,13g

BAGGY SEAT

The key to finding a solution to this problem, illustrated in Fig. II,14b, is in recognizing and defining the posture characteristics. Again, we will address three possible body types, the causes of the baggy seat, and possible solutions.

 A. The first body type labelled "A" in Fig. II,14a appears to lean forward at the waist. This does not mean it is wrong, however. All of us learned from infancy how to walk by ourselves; how to gain balance, and, as we grew, we continued to unconsciously adjust our balance to compensate for muscle mass, etc. Out of this progressive development our own unique posture emerged.

It is easier to see how much this person "stands forward" when she stands with her heels against a wall--both calf and heel may touch the wall, but the buttocks may be a couple inches (several centimeters) away from it.

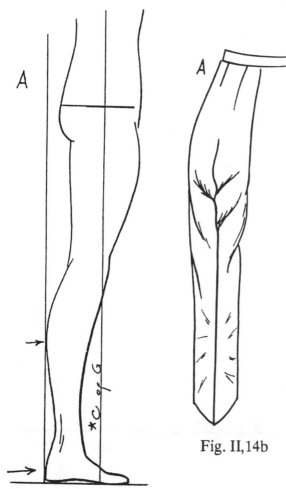

Figure II,14b illustrates what the fitting problems may look like. It is probable that much of the undesirable bagginess is caused by a muscular thigh; the front pants leg is not large enough. So this then is a multiple fitting problem. This body posture may also result in a large calf--the back pants leg is not cut wide enough.

CORRECTION 1: One of the most successful ways to remove all of the bagging is to replace the back Creaseline with a seam (especially when woven fabric is used). Then it is possible to control the amount of fabric under the buttocks by shaping as much or little as you desire. (Suitable for all fabrics.)

Fig. II,14b

Fig. II,14a

The numbers in the following explanation coincide with those shown in Fig. II,14c, d, and e.

1. Cut apart the back pattern along the Creaseline, through the main dart. Allow 1" *(2.5cm)* seams when cutting out the muslin.

2. With the muslin on, shape this seam to your liking taking in under the buttocks (behind the knee) and letting out around the fullness of the calf.

3. Extend the creaseline edges at the heel 1" to 2" *(2.5cm to 5cm)* Compare the profile view of the body to the pattern of the OUTER LEG. Do they appear somewhat similar?

4. In addition to the above, it may be necessary to make the crotch curve deeper and trim the seam to 1/4" or 3/8" *(.6cm or 1cm)*. If the seat of the body seems to "droop," then the back crotch/inseam point should be lowered 1/2" to 3/4" *(1.2cm to 2cm)*--the back inseam will now be stretched when sewn to the front between the knee and the crotch.

5. Redraw and lower the waistline about 1/2" to 3/4" *(1.2cm to 2cm)* to compensate for the amount that was cut from the crotch.

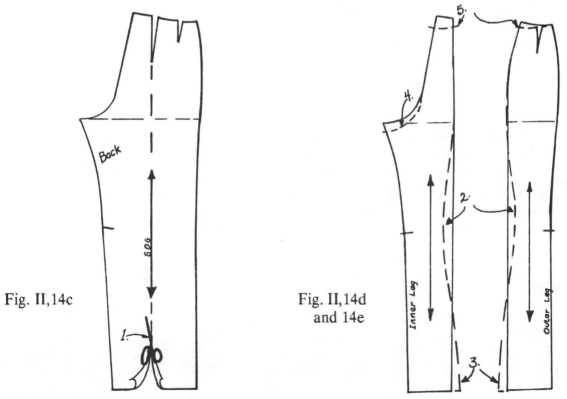

Fig. II,14c

Fig. II,14d
and 14e

CORRECTION 2: This adjustment works nicely on most knits and some wovens if they will take shrink-shaping. Tightly woven gabardines, for example, are very difficult to correct in this way.

The numbers in Fig. II,14f correspond to the following steps:

1. Lower the crotch/inseam point about 3/8" *(1cm)* so that the back inner seam is stretched onto the front between the knee and the crotch; stretching about 5/8" *(1.6cm)*.

2. Shape the side seam and inner seam, reducing the amount of excess fabric under the buttocks (back of knee) the same amount for each side.

3. Shape from the knee level down to the hemline to accommodate the calf; add 1" *(2.5cm)* or more to each side of the pattern at the hemline.

Please note that all the shaping is done to the pattern back to accommodate the back of leg and the posture; no changes are made to the front.

Special handling is needed in sewing these pieces together. The back leg is stretched somewhat along the side seam between the Crotch Depth line and the hemline, but mostly in the area of the curves, for a distance of about 8" *(20cm)* or more to each side of the knee level. Stretching is more easily accomplished with a narrower seam allowance.

Expect to cut off at least 3/4" *(2cm)* from the length of the back leg across the entire width of the hemline. Then pin the inner seams together; stretching the back onto the front.

To complete this process, see "Finishing Touches."

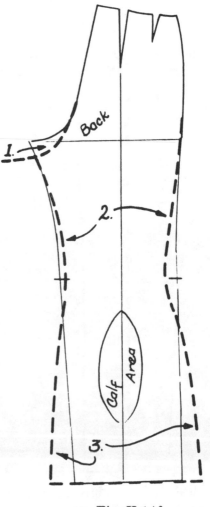

Fig. II,14f

B. The second body type (Fig. II,14g) is quite different from the body structure of "A" in Fig. II,14a. Here the body appears to be standing more vertically; it also has small buttocks. The calf and heel do not extend beyond the seat line as the previous body; the seat protrusion is shallow so that it is necessary to reduce the amount of fabric covering it.

CORRECTION: Because the buttocks are flatter than the average, the pattern will be made flatter, which is accomplished by eliminating some or all of the width in the darts.

The numbers below correspond to the numbers in Fig.II,14h:

1. Leave the darts in the same location, but reduce their width at the waistline. The main dart (long dart) may, in some circumstances, be eliminated altogether--that is, if the buttocks are very flat, the center back seam can absorb the width of the dart and still maintain proper fit.

2. Straighten the center back seam so that it is nearly parallel to the straight of grain (SOG).

3. Inner seam at the crotch needs to be taken in, perhaps 3/4" *(2cm)* or more, and tapered downward to the knee level. Reshape the curve of the crotch seam and trim the seam to 1/4" or 3/8" *(.6cm or 1cm)* before trying on.

4. Some of the excess fabric may also be taken off along the sides.

5. Lower the CB waistline, tapering across to the side seam. If too much is trimmed away, it could result in the back waistline being pulled down when seated, which in turn creates a tightness across the front waistline and discomfort at the crotch seam. Therefore, caution is recommended; lower the CB in small increments--sit testing each 1/4" *(.6cm)* adjustment.

6. There should be no stretching of the back inner seam for this body type.

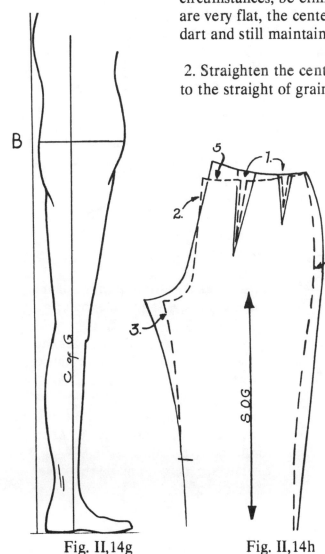

Fig. II,14g   Fig. II,14h

C. The third body (Fig. II,14i) can expect a variety of fitting problems. The buttocks extend more than average. By comparing illustrations, we can see that the body with the flat buttocks would not create crotch smiles; but this one usually does. Because of the buttocks muscle mass, the crotch seam is pulled from the front toward the rear, and undesirable fit in the front is the result.

CORRECTION: Add more width across the back from side seam to side seam, enlarge the width of the main dart, and make a more slanted CB line (as opposed to the vertical CB line used on "B").

The numbers in Fig. II,14j correspond to the numbers in the following steps. The broken line indicates the correction.

1. About half of the width needed across the back will be applied at the Center Back seam.

2. Draw the Center Back seam with more slant, duplicating the body shape (viewed from the side) between buttocks and waistline.

3. The main dart is made wider at the waistline; perhaps both darts may need to be longer as well.

4. Redraw the waistline. Raising the Center Back at least 1/2" *(1.2cm)* above the existing waistline.

5. Add more width to pattern near crotch area tapering to the knee.

To eliminate excess fabric under the buttocks an option might be to make a seam along the Creaseline. Apply the correction used for body type "A" in Fig. II,14d, steps 1, 2, and 3 for making the seam; but since "C" does not have the calf muscle that "A" does, it is not necessary to make the lower leg that shapely

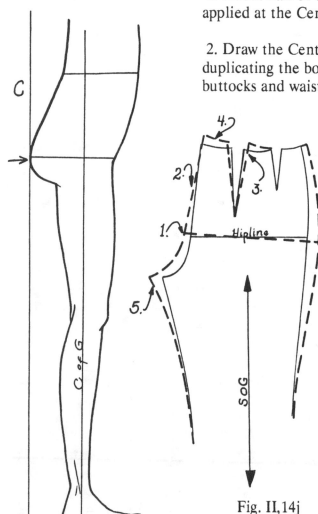

Fig. II,14i

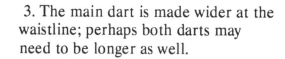

Fig. II,14j

THE MASTER PATTERN

After the adjustments are completed, you should transfer all these lines onto a medium-weight non-woven material. PELLON PLUS® (#40) is very good for this purpose! Because it is easy to see through, it is not necessary to use the tracing wheel and tracing paper method; you can simply pin the PELLON on top of your pattern and trace over it with a fine point felt tip pen. If you decide to draw the cutting line onto your pattern, it may be easier if you use one color for the sewing line and another for the stitching line.

You may cut the PELLON pattern on the cutting line. Pin it onto the fabric, but be careful in cutting so that you don't cut anything off the pattern and thereby destroy the shape and FIT.

This completed master pattern is now ready for many years of reliable service! If you want to design various styles from it, you should make separate fashion patterns--but retain an extra copy of the original.

For instructions on how to make a permanent pattern, refer to Chapter I, Making the Master Pattern.

FINISHING TOUCHES

The finishing touches offered here help the sewer to achieve a more professional appearance. Pressing the pants, using the shrink-shape technique, should be applied to all pants and slacks styles in particular, but may be used successfully on others as well. However, the shaped hemline detail is used almost exclusively for basic pants and slacks where the leg is wide enough at the hemline to be appropriate.

PRESSING PANTS

The technique illustrated here is called **Shrink-Shaping**. It is used to shrink in the fullness of the fabric at the back of the leg. Some fabrics will not respond as well to this treatment as others; but the attempt will make an improvement and is worth the effort. For instance, Polyester Gabardines are nearly impossible to shrink-shape while wool knits respond beautifully. Oftentimes, the problem of too much fabric under the buttocks or at the back of the leg is caused by improper pressing. The presser may have inadvertently stretched the creaseline by running hands firmly along it in order to smooth out the area. The emphasis was focused only on a creaseline without considering the consequence of this simple action--a stretched creaseline.

Immediately after cutting:

 1. Mark the Creaseline on the wrong side of fabric. Hand sew along this line making stitches about 1" *(2.5cm)* in length so that the Creaseline is visible on the face side. Do this on both the front and back parts.

 2. Stitch up pants, OR press the creaseline on each part separately. Because of the personalized fit for bodies with legs that are bowed inward (touching etc.--see "Sags" Reason "B"), it is important to press each piece separately. Then the shrink-shaping technique is done without using the yardstick technique that is described in the following steps.

 3. Pin or baste the inner seams and the side seams together from the hemline up to within about 8" *(20cm)* of crotch.

 4. Lay pants onto ironing board (or other pressing surface) so that the innerseam of one leg is up, pressing each leg separately. Use a yardstick as a guide; lay it alongside the seam and straighten the seam (even though curves were cut into the shaping of the leg).

 5. Secure this straightened seam to the board using wig pins or any oversized pins.

6. Notice the humps along the proposed creaseline in Fig. II,15. This is the fullness we attempt to Shrink-Shape.

7. Hold the steam iron slightly above the hump, allowing the steam to penetrate the fabric. By hand, or clapper, or iron and press cloth, gently force the humps to shrink-in and lie flat.

If a sharper, more permanent crease is desired, dip the press cloth into a mixture of one tsp. white vinegar and one cup of water. Wring out the cloth as much as possible and re-press the crease. This solution is also good for taking out undesirable creases and wrinkles. (Where wrinkles are more stubborn, it may be necessary to gradually increase the vinegar portion to as much as 3 or 4 tablespoons in one cup of water.)

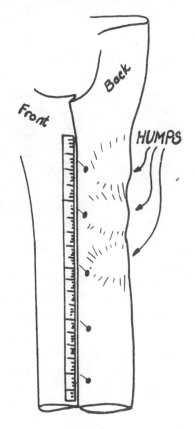

Fig. II,15

Pressing the creaseline and hem should be done after the pants are finished; however, it may be done beforehand if and only if you are sure the width and length of the leg are acceptable. Changing the crease and hem lines is extremely difficult because it shows on many fabrics. Pressing the crease out using the vinegar solution works well most of the time but even that does not always work. (Also used for pleated skirts and seams that won't lie flat.)

PLEASE use a pressing cloth for all pressing done on the face of the fabric.

SHAPED HEMLINE

When the seamstress has cared enough about her image to complete her garment in a professional manner, it in turn makes a statement about the seamstress--she cares! A shaped hemline is part of that statement.

The hemline of slacks and trousers should be shaped with a concave curve in front and a convex curve at the back. The purpose of such shaping is to present a fine finishing touch--a more expensive appearance--a simple yet impressive detail!

This "touch" can be applied to any quality fabric; even adding a nice finish to garments made of relatively inexpensive materials. It may take a little longer to do but the results are worth the effort.

The pant length is determined mainly by the type of shoe and height of heel worn with each garment. The front creaseline should hang without "breaking" (a kink created by the hemline resting on the shoe). The back creaseline should hang longer than the sole part of the heel. In flats, it may mean that the hemline is about 1/2" to 3/4" *(1.2cm to 2cm)* off the floor. In heels, it may mean that the hemline is 3/4" to 1-1/4" *(2cm to 3.7cm)* off the floor. It is your decision; the method of control is the same as shown in Fig. II,16a and 16b. In either case, the front should never be lower than the back.

After determining the hemline length for both front and back, put small crosswise marks at the creaselines (a).

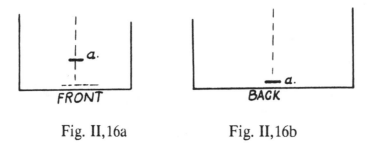

Fig. II,16a   Fig. II,16b

Place pattern pieces together at side seam and faintly draw a guideline between center front and center back. Disconnect the pieces and reconnect them, matching the inner seams. (See Fig. II,16c.)

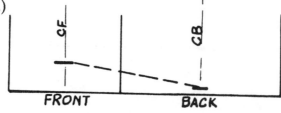

Fig. II,16c

Refine the guidelines into gentle curves by placing the French Curve along the hemline as shown in Fig. II,16d. Concave in the front; convex in the back.

Add only 3/4" to 1" *(2cm to 2.5cm)* maximum for hem allowance.

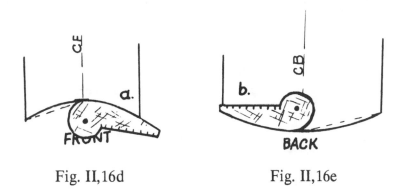

Fig. II,16d   Fig. II,16e

With a shaped hemline, it is recommended that you use the following sequence for construction of the pants:

1. Cut out pants. Use tracing wheel and paper to transfer the notches, darts, waistline, curve of crotch, as well as creasline and hemline accurately before doing any stitching.

2. Carefully machine stitch along the hemline marking of each piece separately. Use contrasting colored thread and long stitches.

3. Slash center front of hem to within 1/8" *(.3cm)* of hemline.

4. Press up hem allowance using machine stitching as the guideline. Also press the Creaseline at this time, applying the Shrink-Shaping technique.

5. Sew up pants. Run basting stitches 1/2" *(1.2cm)* above pressed edge.

6. Finish the hemming by hand or machine. Press firmly again.

7. Remove machine guideline stitching from the hemline.

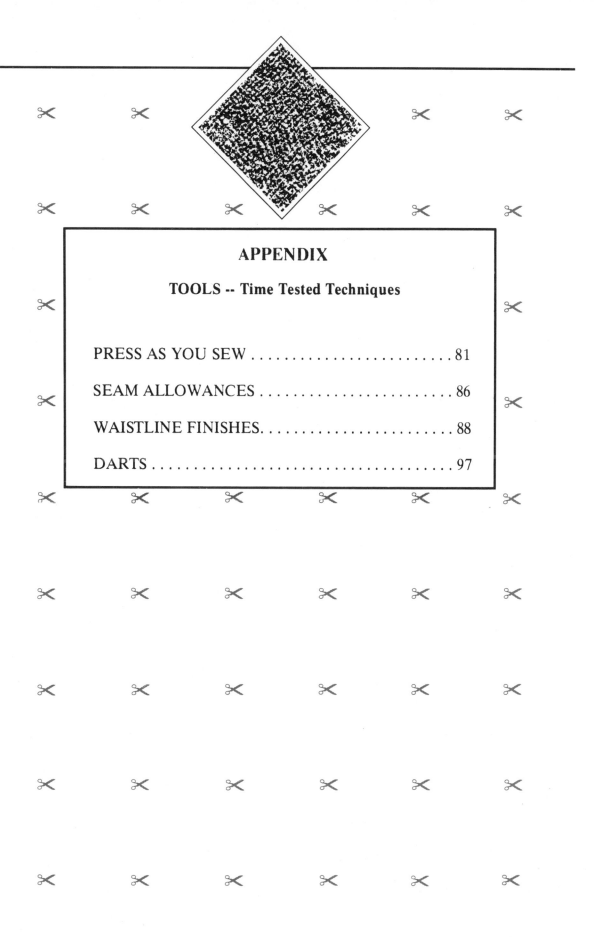

APPENDIX

TOOLS -- Time Tested Techniques

APPENDIX

TOOLS -- Time Tested Techniques

PRESS AS YOU SEW

Unless shape is pressed in as the seams are sewn, as a tailor always does, it is impossible to achieve real satisfaction. Just one final pressing is generally not sufficient. For best results, pressing should be done with the proper equipment. Each dart and seam is stitched and pressed to fit the body curves.

Pressing and ironing are not the same. Pressing is a press/lift- press/lift motion that applies heat and steam, gently so as not to imprint the seam edges; and firmly at specified areas--but never with heavy pressure. Ironing is running the iron over the fabric (with some pressure) in long, back-and-forth strokes, smoothing out large areas to remove wrinkles. Pressing is used more frequently with sewing than is ironing.

Construction pressing begins the moment a pattern envelope is opened. Gently iron the pattern pieces with low, dry heat. Iron woven fabrics wrinkle-free and lightly steam-press knit fabrics before laying them out for cutting. Where possible, remove any creases. If, however, the creases cannot be removed completely, it is advisable to arrange the main pattern pieces, avoiding the creased areas.

There may be fabrics that will not lie straight, even though they were torn or cut on a crossgrain thread. To straighten, pin the straight-of-grain down to a long line marked on the cutting board. Usually, all it takes is a little nudging into place and gentle press/lift (with steam) to get the grain threads to even out. This is an easy way to prepare woolens for matching plaids, checks, and stripes.

Begin pressing with the first seam or dart you make. Darts are intended for use in molding fabric across a body's curves and should be pressed over a curve, not ironed flat. Use a Seam Roll or Dressmaker's Ham for molding darts so that no dimples or creases are inadvertently formed at the points.

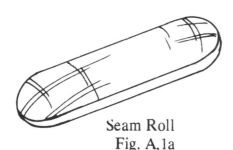

Seam Roll
Fig. A,1a

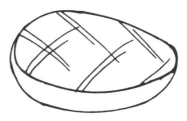

Dressmaker's Ham
Fig. A,1b

DART DIRECTION

Turn the fold of horizontal darts downward; this includes the bust and elbow darts. Turn the fold of vertical darts toward the centers; this includes the shoulder and waistline darts. If the fabric is thick and bulky, it is expedient to slash the wide end of the sewn darts to within about 3/8" *(1cm)* of the point as shown in Fig. A,2; press open and trim away some of the excess fabric. Use CAUTION when pressing darts in order not to imprint the fold or seam edges onto the right side of the fabric. The shape of the Seam Roll helps prevent this, but as an added precaution, lay a strip of brown wrapping paper (or self-fabric) between the seam allowance or hem allowance and the main part of the garment.

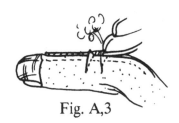

Fig. A,2

Sleeve seams are easy to press open when a Seam Roll is placed inside the sewn sleeve as shown in Fig. A,3. "Kimono" or "Raglan" sleeves may also be shaped over it. If the seam is too curvey, using the Dressmaker's Ham may be more suitable.

Fig. A,3

FITTING PROBLEMS CORRECTED

Pressing as you sew is as important as your sewing. Often, pressing can help to correct a poorly sewn area and can minimize the appearance of a fitting problem--using the proper equipment, of course.

Be aware that fitting problems and perhaps even irreparable damage can be created at the ironing board.

To recall a few instances:
- "Rings" at the point of a bust dart, caused by trying to get the point of the iron to press to the end of the dart on *the ironing board.*
- Knit fabric stretched out of shape at the points of the back skirt darts; created when trying to press the points by laying the skirt over the round end of *the ironing board.*
- Necklines and armholes stretched out of shape while shoulder seams are being pressed open on *the ironing board.*

And this one happens often:

- The hem of a straight skirt (knit) stretched out, looking like a flared skirt, while pressing the hem; caused by letting the fabric encircle *the ironing board.*

Please do not throw out the ironing board! It does have its purpose; but not in construction pressing. In using our pressing equipment, all we really need is a table or a counter top (or ironing board) on which to support a garment. The long side seams of coats, skirts, dresses, and pants are more easily pressed when the long, flat area of a Sleeve Board is used. Slip it under the seam or down into the pants leg--PRESS--and allow the steam to cool and dry before removing. Of course, the Sleeve Board is great for pressing sleeves, too!

SLEEVES

For a "perfect" set-in sleeve, shape-press the cap to fit the armscye before the sleeve is sewn in place.

First, measure around the garment armhole. Next, sew two lines of semi-long stitches along the sleeve cap, 1/4" *(.6cm)* apart; one on the stitching line and the other in the seam allowance. Measure the sleeve cap and draw up the threads until the cap measures the same as the armhole. Fasten threads around pins to secure. Now use the smaller end of a Dressmaker's Ham, which is about the same shape as the top of your shoulder. Stand the ham on the other end in front of you. Pin the center of the top of the sleeve to the top center of the ham as shown in Fig. A,4a (wrong side of fabric up). Fit the cap over the edge of the ham as far as the notches and pin to ham. Evenly distribute the fullness along the stitching.

Fig. A,4a

Press in the fullness of the crown as well as the seam allowance (see Fig. A,4b), being careful not to form little creases in the fabric. The sleeve cap should be pressed one side at a time, removing the pins from the first side in order to pin and press the other side. Preshaping the sleeve cap greatly simplifies the sleeve setting procedure. (For more details, see "Set a Sleeve" in Chapter I.)

Fig. A,4b

COLLARS

Collar seams should be pressed open even though they will be folded and creased along the stitching line. By opening and pressing either straight or curved seams, you are controlling the shape and can prevent seam "wells." Both the straight and the long, curved edge of the Tailor Board, as shown in Fig. A,5a, make corner turning easy; with it any corner be pressed open to the very end.

Fig. A,5a

Use the board unpadded for areas requiring a sharp press, such as collar edges. Use it with the pad for areas you want to remain softer in appearance.

Those hard-to-handle little curves on small collars or on scallops are so easy to work when the seams are pressed open first. Step-grade the seams, trim the corners, turn the collar and press so the seams are rolled slightly to the underside. Open the collar again and stitch the seam allowance along the undercollar to within a inch or so of the corner--as close as you can. (See Fig. A,5b.)

Fig. A,5b

DON'T WORK SO HARD

Avoid using pressure with your steam iron to produce the sharp- edged seam. You are working too hard. Let the steam work for you. Besides, excessive heat is damaging to most fabrics. If steam and pressure are needed for a particular area, then a Clapper should be used.

The Clapper is a smooth piece of hardwood shaped to fit the hand and grooved at the sides for easy handling. (See Fig. A,6.)

To use it:

 1. First apply steam to the garment at the area to be pressed (holding the steam iron slightly above the fabric for a moment or two--allowing the steam to penetrate well).

 2. Using the Clapper, beat the steam into the fabric. Or simply hold the Clapper in position until the area has cooled and dried.

CAUTION: Beating can produce a shine on some fabrics, so try it on a sample first. It might be advisable to use a press cloth between the Clapper and the garment for added protection. Strips of brown wrapping paper (or self fabric) inserted between the seam edges and the garment will help prevent a seam mark.

Areas that usually require the Clapper treatment are:

- The edges and points of lapels and collars.
- The bulky edges of hems at side seams, front coat facings, and slash pockets.

Fig. A,6

These tools are not imperative for your sewing. Only a needle is. But they are necessary if you desire professional-looking results and good fit.

Some of these tools may seem expensive but they are a once-in-a- lifetime investment. Until you can accumulate them all, you might improvise as I did. For several years, I used a tightly rolled magazine covered with muslin in place of a Seam Roll. The ham I made got a little soft and I sewed a little tuck across it. As I could afford it, I replaced my home-made improvisations.

SEAM ALLOWANCE ANALYSIS

Another way to make our sewing look more professional is to vary the widths for seam allowances. Garment manufacturers have used this technique successfully. They use various widths for seam allowances depending upon what type seaming is to be applied and depending upon the shape of the pattern. Does this seem confusing? It may be to the uninformed. The savings to the factory owner, however, is very important--less fabric is used in each garment because the pattern pieces fit together more closely when making the layout. The savings to the machine operator is very important--no excessive time is spent trimming away or clipping curves. These operators earn their money based upon piece-work; efficient ways of handling an item are important to them. Their industry is a marvel in time management and production flow.

In the past you have probably been using patterns that recommend a 5/8" *(1.6cm)* seam allowance all around. While that amount is workable on straight seams or those that are only slightly curved, it is not only difficult to handle on the curvier areas, but also unnecessary. Besides, the instruction sheets that accompany the commercial pattern usually state that seams in certain areas should be trimmed away or clipped in a certain manner--right?

Table A,1 shows the recommended amounts for select areas on the patterns.

Could the commercial pattern companies adopt some of these methods? As much as I believe it to be more efficient and produce better results for the home sewer, I also can see where the change would be a monumental one. Change creates confusion--even if it is in the form of progress. The costs in the conversion of advertising and educational material could be greater than it is worth. To the pattern companies, patterns are still selling just the way they are. The instruction sheets will probably continue to read "trim" and "clip."

Not all pattern companies include the seam allowances. **BURDA** (printed in Offenburg, Germany) furnishes only the stitching lines; permitting the consumer to add the exact seam allowances that he/she considers suitable.

You now have the opportunity to update your knowledge and skills using the exact seam allowance you want, where you want it.

A collar may or may not have shapely curves, depending upon its style. Convertible styles have relatively straight lines and the 5/8" seam allowance is suitable; however, flat styles have curved lines that are not easily handled when it comes time to press and turn the seams to the inside. Therefore, on flat collars, a 1/4" to 3/8" *(.6cm to 1cm)* amount should be used.

TABLE A,1

RECOMMENDED SEAM ALLOWANCES

Armholes - - - - - - - - - - -	3/8"	*(1cm)*
Center Back - - - - - - - - -	5/8" to 3/4"	*(1.6 to 2cm)*
Collars- - - - - - - - - - - - -	1/4" to 3/8"	*(.6 to 1cm)*
Crotch* - - - - - - - - - - - -	1/2" to 5/8"	*(1.2 to 1.6cm)*
Cuffs of sleeves- - - - - - -	3/8"	*(1cm)*
Hems:		
Straight- - - - - - - - - -	2" to 3"	*(5 to 7.5cm)*
Curved - - - - - - - - - -	1" to 2"	*(2.5 to 5cm)*
Necklines- - - - - - - - - - -	1/4" to 3/8"	*(.6 to 1cm)*
Pockets:		
Rounded- - - - - - - - -	1/4" to 3/8"	*(.6 to 1cm)*
Squared- - - - - - - - - -	3/8" to 5/8"	*(1 to 1.6cm)*
Shoulder Seams- - - - - - -	1/2" to 5/8"	*(1.2 to 1.6cm)*
Side Seams:		
Bodice - - - - - - - - - -	1/2" to 5/8"	*(1.2 to 1.6cm)*
Pant - - - - - - - - - - - -	5/8" to 1"	*(1.6 to 2.5cm)*
Skirt - - - - - - - - - - - -	5/8" to 1"	*(1.6 to 2.5cm)*
Topstitching - - - - - - - - -	3/4" to 1"	*(2 to 2.5cm)*

Fabrics that tend to ravel should be cut with the wider of the recommended seam allowances.

*NOTE: The instructions for sewing pants recommends that the crotch seam be trimmed 1/4" *after* stitching, but only in the area of the curves.

WAISTLINE FINISHES

Waistbands vs Facings   - - -   Elastic vs Darts

Several choices are available for finishing waistlines of pants or skirts. The type or style may depend upon the shape of the body it is to fit.

Straight
Fig. A,7

Contour
Fig. A,8

Facing
Fig. A,9

Comparing the illustrations below will assist with the decision. The primary factor to consider is comfort.

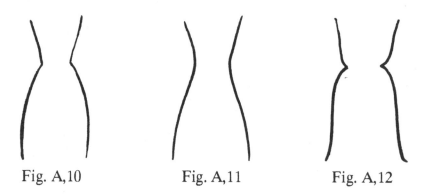

Fig. A,10   Fig. A,11   Fig. A,12

Figure A,10 can wear any style she wants. If STRAIGHT is selected, she should limit the width to about 1-1/4" or 1-1/2" *(3.2cm to 3.7cm)*.

Figure A,11 can also wear all types. She may want to take advantage of her slim torso and wear wider waistbands and perhaps add wide belt carriers, too.

Figure A,12 will be more comfortable with either the CONTOUR or FACING type finishes.

WAISTBAND CONSTRUCTION METHODS

There are several methods shown for the STRAIGHT type waistband. "A" and "B" use interfacing or elastic on a "one piece" band. "C" uses interfacing on a "two piece" band.

The CONTOUR type is always two-piece.

"D" illustrates how to apply FACING for a waistline finish without the band.

The use of elastic is shown in two types of application; "E" in place of a facing, and "F" with a waistband.

STRAIGHT
"One-Piece"

A. This method uses one piece of self (garment) fabric which can be cut to any desired width or length. An "Iron-on" type interfacing can be applied which would eliminate the necessity for using stitching.

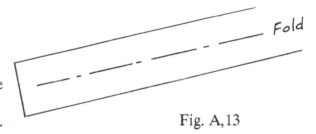

Fig. A,13

Garment fabric: Cut band double the desired finish width and add 1/2" *(1.2cm)* for seam allowance all around.

Interfacing: Cut 5/8" *(1.6cm)* wider than finish width of garment fabric band.

1. Pin interfacing to wrong side of fabric, but to the "front side" of band; 1/4" *(.6cm)* in from the cut edge of band and extending across the fold line by 3/8" *(1cm)*. (See Fig .A,14a.)

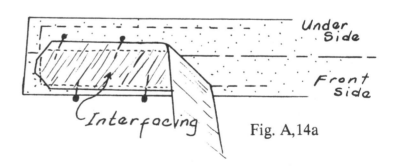

Fig. A,14a

2. Iron on or stitch the interfacing to waistband 1/4" in from edge of interfacing. Trim corners. (See Fig. A,14a.)

3. Fold band lengthwise with right sides together and stitch across the ends as shown in Fig. A,14b. Step-grade seams.

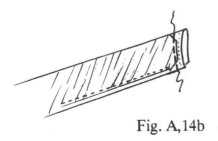

Fig. A,14b

(Figure A,27 at end of this article shows Step-grading.)

B. This method also uses one piece of self fashion fabric and "no-roll" types of interfacing; elastic or woven.

Garment fabric: Cut band double the desired finish width and add 1/2" *(1.2cm)* all around.

Interfacing: Cut interfacing or elastic to desired length.

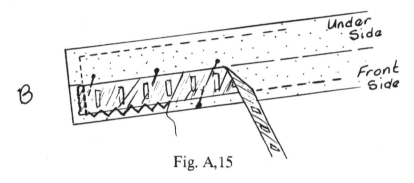

Fig. A,15

1. Pin onto wrong side of fabric (on "front side" of band) placing one edge along the fold line. (See Fig. A,15.)

2. Zig-zag or hand tack the other edge the other edge to the seam line. If elastic is used, be sure to securely stitch the cut ends.

3. Fold the band lengthwise with right sides together and stitch across the ends as shown in Fig. A,14b on previous page. Step-grade seams.

CROSS-CUT VIEW
"One-Piece"

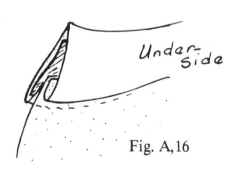

Fig. A,16

STRAIGHT
"Two-Piece"

C. This method is generally used when heavier fabric is involved. The facing is then cut of a light-weight fabric or ribbon.

Garment fabric: Cut band the desired finished width and length and add 1/2" *(1.2cm)* seam allowances all around.

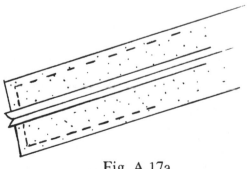

Fig. A,17a

Facing fabric: Cut the same size as garment fabric or use ribbon that is 1" *(2.5cm)* narrower.

Interfacing: Cut 1/2" *(1.2cm)* narrower than the cut width of garment fabric.

1. Pin interfacing to wrong side of garment fabric, 1/4" *(.6cm)* in from edges. (See Fig. A,17b.)

2. Stitch interfacing to waistband 1/4" *(.6cm)* in from edge of interfacing. Trim corners. (See Fig. A,17b.)

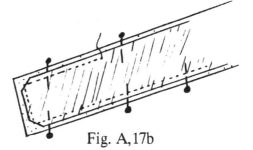

Fig. A,17b

3. Turn the edges under along the seam of the facing material and press. If ribbon is used it is not necessary to turn the edges under.

Fig. A,17c

4. Pin the facing onto right side of band so that the seam allowances will lay together as shown in Fig. A,17c and top-stitch along the facing--very close to the folded edge.

5. Fold band lengthwise (with right sides together) and stitch across the ends. Step-grade seams.

NOTE: The "no-roll" interfacing may be applied at this time using the "B" method in the "One-Piece" waistband.

CROSS-CUT VIEW
"Two-Piece"

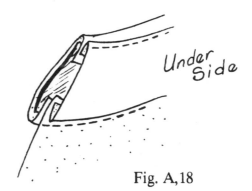

Under Side

Fig. A,18

WAISTBAND CLOSURE
"Overlap/Underlap"

Make either the overlap or underlap extension piece about 1-1/4" *(3cm to 3.2cm)* for both one-piece and two-piece bands. Figure A,19 illustrates the "Underlap" extension.

Fig. A,19

"No-Lap"

The ends of the waistband butt together and are held closed with hook and eye. This method of closure is applied when heavier fabrics would add too much bulk by overlapping. Use strong coat hook and eye for closure.

Some very large hook and eye combinations can be applied to the outside of the garment; they are decorative as well as functional.

Fig. A,20

CONTOUR

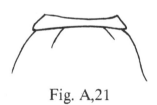

Fig. A,21

This waistband style is always made by the two-piece method. It is curved and therefore rests lower on the waist area than the straight and seems to be more comfortable for those whose back waistline dips downward. You will usually see this band made narrow in front and wide in back.

FACING

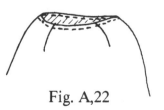

Fig. A,22

D. This type waistline finish is used for eliminating the bulk of a waistband. The body in Fig. A,12 will find it more comfortable than either of the conventional straight methods. Since it is cut to the exact shape of the top of the skirt or pants, it fits very smoothly.

To make a facing pattern:

1. Lay pattern paper across the top of the pattern and trace the sewing lines of the waist, center back, center front, side seams and the darts. (See Fig. A,23a.)

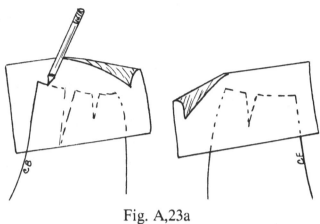

Fig. A,23a

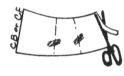

Fig. A,23b   Fig. A,23c

2. Make the facing about 2-1/2" *(6.4cm)* wide. Add seam allowance. Cut around facing pattern. Fold out darts and tape them closed. (See Fig. A,23b.)

3. Trim 1/4" *(.6cm)* from the outer side edge of facing pattern. (See Fig. A,23c.)

Facing fabric: Cut facing from either the fashion garment fabric or other light-weight material.

Stay piece: Cut a piece of pre-shrunk seam binding or twill tape the length of waistline measurement.

To sew to garment:

1. Stitch right sides of garment and facing together along the waistline seam--stretching the facing slightly.

2. Lay the tape or finding over the same waistline stitchine, pinning and easing the garment excess onto the tape. Excess should not be eased across the center back--only along the sides and a small amount across the abdomen. Stitch along the waistline seam. (See Fig. A,23d.)

Fig. A,23d

3. Trim (step-grade) the seam allowances: (See Fig. A,27.)
   Garment side, trim to 3/8" *(1cm)*.
   Facing side, trim to 1/4" *(.6cm)*.

4. Press and understitch the seam to the facing.

5. Turn the facing to the inside of garment and press. Tack the facing down at the seams, darts and the ends to the zipper tape. (See Fig. A,23e.)

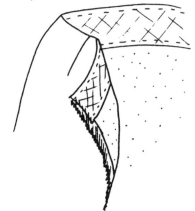

Fig. A,23e

NOTE: The edge of the facing can be finished off at your descretion using the serger, zig-zag stitch or turning it under and stitching with a straight stitch. (The latter is not recommended for stiff or bulky fabrics because the probability exists that a ridge will show when the garment is being worn.)

CROSS-CUT VIEW
"Facing"

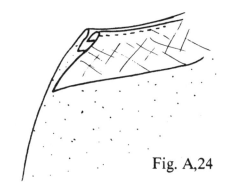

Fig. A,24

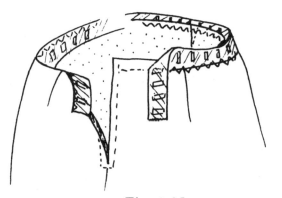

Fig. A,25

ELASTIC

Elastic at the waistline is very comfortable -- and it doesn't have to be in a band or casing. It may be sewn directly onto the pant or skirt in place of a facing.

E. This method is excellent for use with heavier fabrics as it eliminates bulkiness of seams. (It sews up quickly, too!) It is adequate for "everyday" garments and works very well on double knits.

The end result will be, 1.) a waistline that is comfortable because of the elastic, 2.) a garment that fits smoothly over the high hip area and across the abdomen because the fitting darts are used.

"No-roll" types of elastic are the favored choice for this application. However, if you feel it to be a bit too stiff, you might find more comfort in "pajama" elastic--especially if it is to be worn directly against your skin.

Using a zipper or not depends on, a.) hipline vs waistline measurement variation, and b.) the "s-t-r-e-t-c-h-i-n-e-s-s" of the fashion fabric.

Sew up the pants (including the darts) but leave off the waistband and try the garment on to see if it will go up over the hips without an opening. If it doesn't then you should finish the waistline as shown in Fig. A,25 above. If it does, then a zipper is not needed and you can proceed with the following.

F. Method for making the circular elastic waistband.

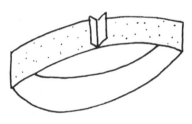

Fig. A,26a

Garment Fabric: Cut 2-1/2" *(6.2cm)* wide and 1" *(2.5cm)* longer than the waistline measurement. Cut the length of this band the stretchiest way of the fabric--and it doesn't matter whether it is lengthwise or crosswise. Stitch the ends together to form a circle.

Elastic: Cut 3/4" *(2cm)* wide elastic the same length as the waist measurement. Stitch the ends together, overlapping them about 3/4" to form a circle. (See Fig. A,26a above.)

Test the snuggness of the elastic by trying it on over your hips. Adjust as needed for your waistline comfort.

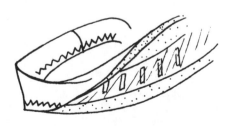

Fig. A,26b

1. Place the elastic circle inside the fabric circle and fold the fabric over to encase the elastic. Zig-zag it closed using a 1/2" *(1.2cm)* seam allowance. (See Fig. A,26b.)

Maybe you should try it over those hips just one more time. If it is still acceptable, you can stitch the band onto the garment.

2. Use only ONE row of zig-zag that is as wide as possible and about 16 stitches to the inch. Stretch the seam as you sew.

There will be three raw edges. (Figure A,26c shows a cross-cut view of the completed procedure.) Since double knits don't ravel it is not necessary to enclose or finish them.

CROSS-CUT VIEW
"Circular band"

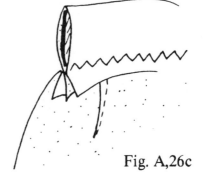

Fig. A,26c

Illustration for Step-grading seams.

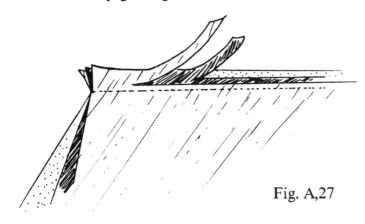

Fig. A,27

DARTS

SHAPED DARTS

Darts are one of the most important elements in achieving fit. They are used to mold fabric over a body curve and proper configuration is vital; where function is seldom given its due credit. Generally, there are four types of darts based upon configuration of the sides and each has its own unique characteristics and consequent locations.

STRAIGHT, CONCAVE, CONVEX, AND COMBINATION

Straight

As its name suggests, the sides are drawn straight down from the edge to the point. Straight darts are used on the skirt back (nearest the zipper), on the back bodice at the waistline up to the mid-back, and on the sleeves at the elbow. In most cases, they may be used on the front bodice for the side bust dart; however, there are body shapes that require individual attention and the combination dart may be more useful. (See Table A,3 for dart width guideline.) Figure A,28 shows a straight dart, sewn directionally, from edge to the point.

Fig. A,28

Concave

Concave darts are used on the front bodice, from the waistline up toward the bust point (Apex). (See Fig. A,29.) As its name suggests, the sides curve away from the fold of the dart--the garment will fit closer to the body and the concave area directly beneath the bosom. Refer to Figs. A, 36a, 36b, and 36c for further details of positioning for the underbust dart.

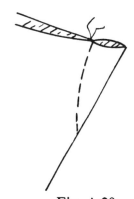

Fig. A,29

Convex

The sides of convex darts curve inward toward the fold. (See Fig. A,30.) They are used on the back bodice at the shoulder, on the front and back of skirts and pants. They may be curved more or less, depending upon the particular need.

Fig. A,30

Combination Concave/Convex

Combination darts are used on the back skirt (the main dart) for shaping into the hollow of a swayed back. It may also replace the straight side dart for the woman whose bosom is more bulbous. (See Fig. A,31.) (See Table A,3 for dart width information.)

The sides of Combination darts curve away from the fold at the edge but gradually curve inward toward the point.

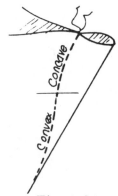

Fig. A,31

Once fit has been established with the proper sized and shaped dart, any dart can be artfully converted into gathers or seams. INTRODUCTION TO DESIGN shows how to easily accomplish these and other basic, yet fashionable, styles.

SKIRT DARTS

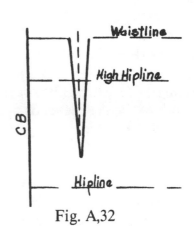

Fig. A,32

Dart width at the waistline is determined by the amount the buttocks extend. For a flat or average extension, make the dart width 1/2" to 1" *(1.2cm to 2.5cm)*; for additional extension, 1-1/2" *(3.7cm)*. (See Fig. A,32.)

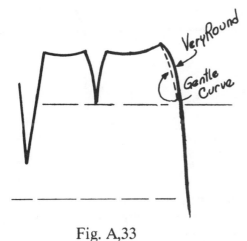

Fig. A,33

The side back dart is positioned midway between Main Dart and Side Seam. (See Fig. A,33.)

Total width of the dart at waistline will vary from 1/2" to 1" *(1.2cm to 2.5cm)* and will be straight or convex, depending upon the amount of curvature of the flesh in that area. (See Fig. A,33.)

Modification for larger buttocks. On some bodies, it may be necessary to shape the CB seam in order to achieve a smooth fit between Hipline and Waistline without making the main dart overly large and abrupt at the point. The fitting session will best help you decide whether the main dart can be made a little bit wider without producing an unwanted bubble at the point or whether better fit is produced with the CB seam is shaped as shown. The key to fit for this body is to avoid extremes; not too large a dart or too severe an angle on the CB seam. Notice also that the sketch shows the waist of the center back is higher than the side. (See Fig. A,34.) Even though with a visual observation of the body we see that the waistline is level, the Back Waist to Floor measurement can be an inch or more longer than the front because of the amount that the buttocks extends.

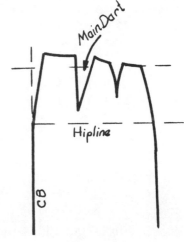

Fig. A,34

BUST DARTS

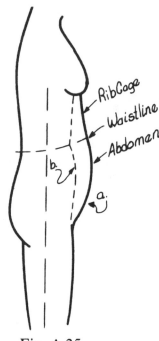

Underbust Dart. The centerline is usually drawn straight down from the Apex, parallel to the CF, beginning 1-1/4" *(3.2cm)* below the Apex. The shape and width of the dart depends upon the size of the bosom and the abdomen.

a. The body type depicted in Fig. A,35 will have a different shaping to the underbust dart, and it might even be necessary to eliminate this dart totally.

b. The body type shown here by the broken line has a small rib cage and will have a larger underbust dart.

Fig. A,35

Expect to make adjustments based upon the results of a fitting session. Fig. A,36a illustrates the shape for the average bosom; Fig. A,36b for the bulbous bosom (size C cup or greater); and Fig. A,36c for large (thick waist) abdomen regardless of the cup size. (See Table A,2 on the following page for recommended underbust dart sizes.)

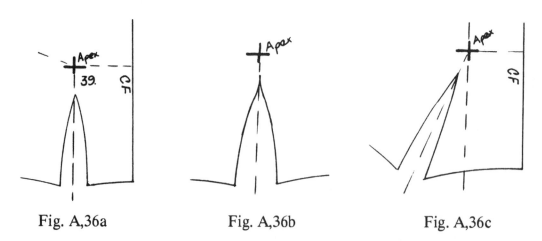

Fig. A,36a   Fig. A,36b   Fig. A,36c

The dart in Fig. A,36c allows the excess fabric to be removed from the side of the abdomen; because it is angled toward the side its width can be enlarged or reduced without causing an overly snug fit across the abdomen.

The tables below give suggested amounts applicable for both underbust and side bust darts. These are to be used as guidelines. The final amounts are determined during a fitting session and depend upon the torso configuration.

TABLE A,2
Width of Bodice Waistline Dart
as a function
of Abdomen and Bra Cup Size

Abdomen	Bra Size			
	A, B or C		D or Larger	
	Inch	Cm	Inch	Cm
Flat	1-1/2	3.7	2 - 2-1/2	5 - 6.7
Rounded	1/2	1.2	1 - 1-1/2	2.5 - 4

TABLE A,3
Width of Side Bust Dart
as a function of
Bra Cup Size

Cup Size	Total Dart Width	
	Inches	Centimeters
A	1	2.5
B	1-1/2	3.7
C	2	5
D	2-1/2	6.2
DD	3	7.5
EE	3-1/2	8.8

INDEX

FITTING PROBLEMS AND THEIR CORRECTIONS

PERSONAL PATTERNS By Jinni - A Manual for Perfect Patternmaking $36.95
(over 300 pages)   Please add $4.00 for mailing.

"This is one of the most comprehensive works for patternmaking and fitting available on the market today." -- Sew It Seams magazine.

"Here's a useful book for home-sewing enthusiasts who want to make beautiful and well-fitting clothes." -- "Profusely illustrated with high-quality black and white drawings." -- JMM, BOOKLIST, American Library Association.

Jinni explains how each body has its own unique shape, posture and proportions that may or may not conform to the standards set by the commercial pattern companies. The reader is given two options for making a "sloper" (a sort of blueprint). In either case you are guided every step of the way by following clearly detailed, step-by-step illustrations -- about 335 in all! Additional features are treatments of grainline and how it can be used for effect or purpose, and the continually overlooked yet vital subject of fit coordination between layers of clothing. From setting sleeves to determining the widths of seams; from positioning pockets to determining button placement; from proper ease amounts for each specific area of the body bto how-to make custom-fit shoulder pads; from eliminating seams and darts to what-to-do when gaining weight and what NOT to do to the patterns when losing weight; from advice to the sewing professional to encouragement for the novice -- and more -- much more!!
ISBN # 0-942003-00-4

OTHER BOOKS by Jinni

-- SKIRTS - Fit and Design $14.95   (over 120 pages)

How to measure and draft or alter a pattern for any body type and achieve perfect results every time. This book shows you easy, yet accurate, methods for making various styles and for using Grainline to enhance the beauty of your designs -- plaids and stripes, too! Every teacher and student will appreciate the clarity of instructions and detailed illustrations that make this edition the primer for all designing. ISBN #: 0-942003-30-6

-- CHOOSING A PATTERN $14.95   (over 95 pages)

Learn how to choose the correct size pattern from your favorite brand of patterns. Learn the differences between balance and proportion; between basic, sloper, master pattern, and sheath. The major pattern companies such as Vogue, Butterick, McCall's, Kwik Sew, Stretch & Sew, and Burda are researched and analyzed. This book reveals facts that have never been disclosed to the general public. ISBN #: 0-942003-10-1

-- FITTING PROBLEMS
And Their Corrections $14.95   (over 120 pages)

From adjusting for the growing body, to what to do about sleeves that are too tight, uneven hemlines, gapping necklines, folds in forward armpit, armhole and back wrinkles. What to do for weight loss or gain -- and what NEVER to do -- and more -- much more! ISBN #: 0-942003-15-2

-- PANTS - Fit and Design $14.95   (over 110 pages)

Pants!! Corrections for smiles, sags, bulges, and baggy seats and why they occur. This book shows how to measure and draft your own pattern -- applying observations about areas of the body that determine how well the pants will fit. Also how to make other styles for slacks, jeans and culottes. And how to make patterns for pockets and yokes; waistbands and other waistline finishes; and correct pressing, too! ISBN #: 0-942003-25-X

-- INTRODUCTION TO DESIGN $14.95   (over 120 pages)

A short course on flat pattern designing. Showing simple and easy ways to make fashionable styles without the hassle of fitting. Follow the step-by-step complete instructions and the perfect-fitting results are guaranteed to be satisfying and exciting. Make several styles of Skirts, Sleeves, Bodices and Shifts -- with information on changing the Grainline of patterns, cutting Off-grain and using proper seam allowances. The vital, yet overlooked (until now) subject of Fit Coordination is explained in detail. ISBN #: 0-942003-20-9

If you are unable to locate these books locally, you may order directly from PERSONAL PATTERNS, P.O. BOX 12093, Bothell, WA 98012-9102, USA. Enclose Money Order or Check and include $2.50 for postage and handling for the first title and $1.00 for each additional title on the same order. Canadian and foreign orders in US funds, please.

(Washington state residents add current Sales Tax amount.)

PERSONAL PATTERNS by Jinni

I want to order:	Quantity	Cost Each	Total Price
CHOOSING A PATTERN	_____	$ 14.95	_$_____
FITTING PROBLEMS And Their Corrections	_____	$ 14.95	_$_____
INTRODUCTION TO DESIGN	_____	$ 14.95	_$_____
PANTS - Fit And Design	_____	$ 14.95	_$_____
SKIRT - Fit And Design	_____	$ 14.95	_$_____
PERSONAL PATTERNS By Jinni - A Manual	_____	$ 36.95	_$_____
for Perfect Patternmaking ($4.00 P&H)		Postage and Handling	_$_____
		TOTAL AMOUNT	_$_____

Allow 2 to 3 weeks for delivery.

Visa or MasterCard #_____ Exp. date:_____

Checks and Money Orders in U.S. Funds, please. Include $2.50 for postage and handling
for the first title and $1.00 for each additional title on the same order.
(Washington state residents add current Sales Tax amount.)

Name:_____

Address:_____

City:_____ State:_____ Zip:_____

*If for some reason I am not satisfied with any book I understand that I may return it
within 2 weeks for a full money-back refund.*

PERSONAL PATTERNS by Jinni

I want to order:	Quantity	Cost Each	Total Price
CHOOSING A PATTERN	_____	$ 14.95	_$_____
FITTING PROBLEMS And Their Corrections	_____	$ 14.95	_$_____
INTRODUCTION TO DESIGN	_____	$ 14.95	_$_____
PANTS - Fit And Design	_____	$ 14.95	_$_____
SKIRT - Fit And Design	_____	$ 14.95	_$_____
PERSONAL PATTERNS By Jinni - A Manual	_____	$ 36.95	_$_____
for Perfect Patternmaking ($4.00 P&H)		Postage and Handling	_$_____
		TOTAL AMOUNT	_$_____

Allow 2 to 3 weeks for delivery.

Visa or MasterCard #_____ Exp. date:_____

Checks and Money Orders in U.S. Funds, please. Include $2.50 for postage and handling
for the first title and $1.00 for each additional title on the same order.
(Washington state residents add current Sales Tax amount.)

Name:_____

Address:_____

City:_____ State:_____ Zip:_____

*If for some reason I am not satisfied with any book I understand that I may return it
within 2 weeks for a full money-back refund.*

PERSONAL PATTERNS by Jinni

I want to order:	Quantity	Cost Each	Total Price
CHOOSING A PATTERN	_____	$ 14.95	_$_____
FITTING PROBLEMS And Their Corrections	_____	$ 14.95	_$_____
INTRODUCTION TO DESIGN	_____	$ 14.95	_$_____
PANTS - Fit And Design	_____	$ 14.95	_$_____
SKIRT - Fit And Design	_____	$ 14.95	_$_____
PERSONAL PATTERNS By Jinni - A Manual	_____	$ 36.95	_$_____
for Perfect Patternmaking ($4.00 P&H)		Postage and Handling	_$_____
		TOTAL AMOUNT	_$_____

Allow 2 to 3 weeks for delivery.

Visa or MasterCard #_____ Exp. date:_____

Checks and Money Orders in U.S. Funds, please. Include $2.50 for postage and handling
for the first title and $1.00 for each additional title on the same order.
(Washington state residents add current Sales Tax amount.)

Name:_____

Address:_____

City:_____ State:_____ Zip:_____

*If for some reason I am not satisfied with any book I understand that I may return it
within 2 weeks for a full money-back refund.*

place

stamp

here

PERSONAL PATTERNS by Jinni
P.O. Box 12093
Bothell, WA   98012

place

stamp

here

PERSONAL PATTERNS by Jinni
P.O. Box 12093
Bothell, WA   98012

place

stamp

here

PERSONAL PATTERNS by Jinni
P.O. Box 12093
Bothell, WA   98012